William Wordsworth

AND THE

Mind of Man

The Poet as Thinker

William Wordsworth

AND THE

Mind of Man

The Poet as Thinker

JOHN O. HAYDEN

Bibli O'Phile Publishing Company
New York, New York

Distributed by E. P. Dutton,
a division of Penguin, USA

BY THE SAME AUTHOR

The Romantic Reviewers 1802–1824 (1969)
Sir Walter Scott: The Critical Heritage (1970)
Romantic Bards and British Reviewers (1971)
William Wordsworth: The Poems (1977)
Polestar of the Ancients: The Aristotelian Tradition
    in Classical and English Literary Theory (1979)
Inside Poetry Out: An Introduction to Poetry (1983)
William Wordsworth: Selected Prose (1988)

Printed on acid free paper

Published by Bibli O'Phile Publishing Company
170 East 61st Street, New York, New York 10021

Frontis:
William Wordsworth, 1831
Wilkin, Francis William
British(?), dates not available
Charcoal & white chalk on brown paper
28⅝ × 18½ in.
Gift of the Estate of Mrs. James T. Fields
Courtesy of Museum of Fine Arts, Boston   06/92

Printed in the United States of America

Library of Congress Catalog Card Number: 92-74987

ISBN: 0-942104-04-8

First Edition

Distributed by E. P. Dutton, a division of Penguin, USA

10   9   8   7   6   5   4   3   2   1

This Book is for
Mary, Michael, Jack, Mark, and Ann

PREFACE

Even though there is an enormous area of agreed understanding about Wordsworth, every reader of his works, certainly every Wordsworthian scholar, has his own Wordsworth. It is, moreover, the nature of literary scholars that they share their views of the writers they deal with, as I am attempting to share mine here: Despite the emotional power that informs so much of what he produced, Wordsworth seems to me an intellectual poet, not of course in the popular sense of one who ponders esoteric philosophical works (although he did his share of that), but in the true sense of one who is curious about everything he runs across, questions the truth of everything, and thinks constantly about it. Wordsworth for me, in other words, was a great thinker, a man who was not afraid to use the ideas of others when useful, but who was profoundly original, as I hope the following pages will help to prove.

I did not, however, come to this view wholly on my own. I had the great good fortune as an undergraduate to take a course on Romantic Literature from Donald Davie, who brought fresh insights to everything he dealt with. More specifically, the pattern concerned with joy that I develop in the last chapter was originally the result of his close reading of Wordsworth. Another scholar, George Dekker, who attended the same class and is now on the faculty of Stanford University, was also very helpful in generously giving advice on my work.

As for my general procedures, I have eschewed the trendy modern methodologies with their annoying jargon and questionable procedures in favor of a more traditional scholarly approach that relies on sound evidence, especially Wordsworth's own works. I have, moreover, tried to address a more general reader rather than a group of specialists. With this in mind, I have provided more intellectual background than is strictly required by specialists; I am myself never annoyed to be reminded of such material by others when not over-done. In the same fashion I have tried to write clearly and engagingly, without writing down. I have attained, I hope, a more relaxed, less stuffy style—again to be more appealing and accessible to a wider readership.

The danger of such a style and fuller background is that the extent to which I have broken new ground may be obscured. In many instances I was working in areas in which little or no work has ever been done, and there-fore from a scrutiny of *primary* evidence I managed to propose many new ways to look at Wordsworth, al-though I trust my notes will demonstrate the thorough-ness of my research.

The central part of this study was researched and written during a year-long sabbatical funded partly by a generous grant from the American Council of Learned Societies. I would like to thank Marilyn Gaull, editor of *The Wordsworth Circle*, for supporting my application for that grant. I would further like to acknowledge the per-mission of the editor of *Studies in Philology* to reprint an article which formed the basis of Chapter 2.

I would also like to thank the Trustees of the Dove Cottage Library, Grasmere, for allowing me to examine manuscripts under their care. My thanks, moreover, to the staffs of the Reading Room of the British Museum and the Shield's Library of the University of California, Davis, who made research an easier and more enjoyable task.

John O. Hayden
Davis, California

CONTENTS

Contents

VI
Wordsworth's Psychology of Vision: Joy, Calm, and Insight

Index

William Wordsworth

AND THE

Mind of Man

The Poet as Thinker

I

Introduction: Wordsworth and "the Mind of Man"

William Wordsworth praised Thomas Gray's "Epitaph upon his Mother, where [Gray] says, 'she was the careful[,] tender Mother of many Children, one of whom alone had the misfortune to survive her' "; Wordsworth admired what he called its "searching thought."[1] But then he wrote, reversing himself completely, that the thought was "wholly out of place"; only in the case of a helpless child would the thought have been appropriate, except under such extraordinary circumstances that it would have been "too peculiar" for a monument. But Wordsworth was only warming up for the final onslaught:

> But in an ordinary case, for a Man permanently and conspicuously to record that this was his fixed feeling; what is it but to run counter to the course of nature, which has made it matter of

1

expectation and congratulation that Parents should die before their Children? What is it, if searched to the bottom, but lurking and sickly selfishness?

What, indeed, does it finally show but the author's "morbid constitution of . . . feelings" and "his deficiency in judgment"?

The extraordinary certainty of Wordsworth's criticisms here concerning emotions, judgment, and normalcy, especially in such a delicate area, demonstrates both his characteristic forthrightness as well as his psychological ability to cut to the heart of the matter, an ability that is so ingrained, so habitual, that he has no doubt of what he says. Such assurance is the result of many years of psychological probing, both of himself and of others.

That William Wordsworth was very interested in psychology can hardly be doubted. Even if one ignored the manifold evidence in his poetry and prose, there are the explicit statements: "The Mind of Man" Wordsworth called "My Haunt, and the main region of my song" (Prospectus to *The Excursion*, lines 40–41). But the extent of his interest and the shapes it took have never been the subject of a full-length study.

It would be perhaps worthwhile from the start to describe the limits I have set in this study. First of all, this is not an examination of Wordsworth's relationship to modern psychology, nor a demonstration of how much Wordsworth did or did not prefigure current thought. Nor, reversing that procedure, is it a study of Wordsworth's debt to past psychological thought, although some effort in that direction is necessary if only to free him from false and misleading entanglements. This is not even a study of what Wordsworth's contemporaries understood his psychological views to be; in fact they seem to have attracted remarkably little attention.

This is rather a study of Wordsworth on his own terms as a writer more than usually interested in "the Mind of Man." Such a focus has never before been attempted, despite Wordsworth's own public insistence, possibly because all literature deals with human experience, especially its psychological dimensions. In fact, it is just this wide experiential psychology that Wordsworth was so fascinated with, rather than such systematic psychology as existed at the time.

Indeed, Wordsworth seems to have abjured scientific psychology altogether—the science that explored the "world within," as the Wanderer in *The Excursion* put it, and that "analyzed/ The thinking principle" and viewed everything "unremittingly / In disconnexion dead and spiritless; / And still dividing, and dividing still, / Break down all grandeur, . . . waging thus / An impious warfare with the very life / Of our own souls!"[2] The Wanderer, usually considered a mouthpiece for the poet, here contemns any systematically analytical or scientific study of the mind.

Science works by both induction and deduction, framing hypotheses or theories from observed data and then examining more data to further validate the theories and to expand them in a cumulative systematic process. Wordsworth, on the other hand, seems to have displayed only a mild interest in systematic psychological theory, being rather, like many of us, fascinated by the make-up of individuals and by individual behavior and motivations. He was not unscientific in his scrutiny of experience, however; he was in fact dedicated to the givens of experience; but he seems to have had little interest in generating large theoretical structures, nor to have been hampered by them, for that matter. Put another way, Wordsworth was a poet almost obsessed with psychology; he was not a psychologist who happened to be a poet.

Another concrete example of his consuming interest in psychology, which he shared to some extent with his sister, occurred on their 1803 tour of Scotland and is registered by Dorothy in her description of the principals in Wordsworth's poem, "The Matron of Jedborough and Her Husband":

> She was a most remarkable person; the alacrity with which she ran up-stairs when we rung the bell, and guessed at, and strove to prevent, our wants was surprizing; she had a quick eye, and keen strong features, and a joyousness in her motions. . . . I found afterwards that she had been subject to fits of dejection and ill-health: *we then conjectured* that her overflowing gaiety and strength might in part be attributed to the same cause as her former dejection. (Italics added)[3]

The mutual conjecturing about the old woman—whom today we would call a manic-depressive—is indicative, I believe, of their constant interest in psychological phenomena, reflected both in her journals and his poetry.

But, regardless of Wordsworth's honesty to experiential truth, he was of course an amateur, not a professional. That is, Wordsworth was highly interested in psychology in the way most thinking people are in a more moderate way, especially people who are interested in literature. And his interest was deliberate: in 1831 he exhorted a would-be poet "to devote hours and hours to the study of human nature, in books, in life, and in [your] own mind. . . ."[4]

Wordsworth himself, as well as his correspondent, could be "amateur" psychologists then more easily than today, could speculate with fewer inhibitions, because there was at that time no "professional" psychology to speak of, for psychology as we know it today began in the late nineteenth century. It is also good to remember that an amateur is not necessarily a dilettante, a meaning it has largely assumed in the past century or so, nor someone who has only a passing interest in psychology; nor is an amateur necessarily less accurate in his observations or conclusions than professionals. The squabbles among the various psychological schools existing since it has been possible to talk about professional psychologists should make it obvious that even today psychology is a science in only a limited sense, for it has no large body of universally accepted theory.

Psychology, in any event, is the one, central interest of Wordsworth under which can be gathered all his other interests. For although scholars usually attempt to catch everything in the net of Wordsworth's philosophical views, his metaphysics and epistemology, it is actually Wordsworth's psychology that connects those views with his literary and creative theory, his general and incidental psychological observations, his social and political concerns, and his visionary probings. An investigation of his psychology consequently allows us to see all these other interests in an organic whole. The problem usually is that we try to see Wordsworth's thought in exactly the way he abhorred—as a collection of fragments.

Wordsworth was keenly interested in "the Mind of Man," and the interest spread through everything he

wrote and took many forms. And the psychological interest was not completely self-directed, as might be suggested by John Keats' phrase, "the wordsworthian or
egotistical sublime," with its accompanying appeal for
a poet without character, identity, or even self.[5] Wordsworth, indeed, had a self that fascinated him, as all
things psychological did, but he didn't stop there, as
Keats himself recognized in preferring him to Milton,
who "did not think into the human heart, as Wordsworth has done."[6] On the one side, his introspection
was thus not merely an egotistical concern, sublime or
otherwise: and on the other side, interest in the psychology of others pervades his work. Few of his poems
contain no psychology and many contain little else.

Psychological analysis of individual experiences and
people occur fairly clearly in a number of works for
which no other reading makes much sense—"Strange
Fits of Passion," "Anecdote for Fathers," "The Thorn,"
and *The Borderers.* In the case of the last three of these,
Wordsworth even supplies the reader with additional
psychological information to avoid misunderstandings.
But in other works the psychology is somewhat obscure
and in need of explanation, and the meaning will be
missed if the reader is not alert to Wordsworth's psychological penchant—for example, in "Simon Lee"—as I
intend to demonstrate in a later chapter.

Occasionally the only clue is a subsequent private
comment, usually in a letter of explanation to a puzzled
friend. One sonnet with such a circumstance—"With
Ships the Sea was Sprinkled"—will be dealt with in a
later chapter. Another example occurs in a late conversation with Aubrey de Vere in which Wordsworth explains that Sir Walter Scott has misquoted "Yarrow Unvisited." Wordsworth insists that the swan in the lines,

"The Swan on still St.Mary's Lake / Floats double, swan
and shadow," could not have been plural:

> The scene when I saw it, with its still and dim
> lake, under the dusky hills, was one of utter lone-
> liness; there was *one* swan, and one only, stem-
> ming the water, and the pathetic loneliness of the
> region gave importance to the one companion of
> that swan, its own white image in the water. It
> was for that reason that I recorded the Swan and
> the Shadow. Had there been many swans and
> many shadows, they would have implied nothing
> as regards the character of the scene; and I should
> have said nothing about them.[7]

Considering that we have this piece of detailed psychological background only because Scott had misquoted
the lines, we can only wonder how many seemingly insignificant details in Wordsworth's poems have so much
observation and thought behind them.

It is just this observation and thought that accounts
so much for the interest of Wordsworth's ideas, for truth
to observation and energy of thought led him to recon-
sider human experience and the accumulated "truths"
about it and hence into the region of paradox. There
was, however, no central paradox to Wordsworth's psychology, but rather the freshness of his scrutiny was
constantly turning up the awful reality underlying the
appearance of things. His metaphysics and epistemology were themselves both, as we shall shortly discuss,
based on paradox—that the world exists but that we
must "create" it and that our minds are both active and
passive. On the road to Vision, moreover, we must, paradoxically, distinguish in order to relate and the joy in-

volved in Vision does not take the form of joy we usually
think of and it operates in the future more than in the
present. And the individual psychological insights in
poem after poem bristle with paradoxes and even infect
his style with oxymorons. Wordsworth was a great
thinker, and, what is more, he was a great original
thinker.

Wordsworth's interest in the mind, moreover, takes
us into further areas that we would not ordinarily think
of as psychological. On one side the psychological
shades off into the spiritual. As I intend to demonstrate,
the psychology of social bonding in the Community of
Natural Piety leads into larger spiritual communities
where there is no separation between animate and inanimate or between the living and the dead. Such is not,
of course, a surprising development in a poet with transcendental aspirations and beliefs.

The visionary experiences likewise connected with
those beliefs were the subject of the ultimate of Wordsworth's psychological investigations, for as usual he was
not content merely to experience vision but wished to
understand the psychology involved, using his own experiences, as well as Coleridge's, as evidence. These
spiritual matters may seem far afield, yet Wordsworth
did clearly probe them, and he himself made no clear-
cut distinction between the psychological and the spiritual. Jonathan Bishop has claimed that Wordsworth's
well-known "spots of time" in *The Prelude* were not
mystical but only psychological phenomena; they were
in fact both at once.[8]

On the side opposite the spiritual, psychology
shades off into epistemology. Or perhaps it would be
more accurate to say that epistemology, the philosophy
of how man knows things, shades off or evolves into

psychology; for before Wordsworth's time the history of psychology was mostly a history of epistemology. And of course epistemology depends to a large extent on metaphysics, for what kind of a world we see ourselves inhabiting determines how the mind can work in knowing it.

Wordsworth was not a philosopher, either in metaphysics or epistemology, in the sense of a developer or follower of a system, yet at the end of the eighteenth century an educated man like Wordsworth had to make choices, for traditional views had been upset by philosophers like John Locke. Still it is good to remember that Wordsworth began with experiences, not with theories; he was not apparently interested in theories per se but only as explanations of those experiences—a point that I don't believe could be made confidently about his friend Coleridge. And the experiences are always worth more to Wordsworth than the explanations—a point that keeps his poetry concrete where others', like Shelley's, is abstract and vague.

The history of Wordsworth's philosophical beliefs, in any case, is well known; in fact, it is the side of Wordsworth most scrutinized and consequently it requires only the barest rehearsal here. The epistemological systems available to Wordsworth were essentially two-fold: the dominant Lockean empirical sensationalism on the one side and on the other the transcendental intuitionism of Plato and the Neoplatonists, the Scottish Intuitionists, and the emergent German school. What was largely at stake was the question whether the mind was active or passive—no small consideration. Was the universe essentially dead and were our minds at its mercy as the source of all knowledge? Or did the universe actively work on us and did the mind shape the universe, at least to some extent?

When Wordsworth's friend, Samuel Taylor Coleridge, was confronted with the choice, he first accepted the sensationalist view of the passive mind but eventually rejected it and posited a compromise between a dualist metaphysic and an intuitionist epistemology in a kind of paradox: objects exist independently of us but we have to "create" them with our minds.[9] Wordsworth's later position was generally in agreement with his friend, except that while Coleridge emphasized the intuitionist side, the active powers of the mind, Wordsworth was closer to the center in accepting a mind that was *both* active and passive.

Wordsworth, that is, found unacceptable the Lockean view that reality exists only outside the mind and that the mind is a passive receptor. The visionary experience itself, moreover, seemed to indicate that the mind was active. And so, like Coleridge, he rejected the sensationalist principle that the mind was totally (or even predominately) passive. On the other hand, unlike Coleridge, he couldn't exclude nature and her effect on the mind; he could not, that is, join in Coleridge's assertion in "Dejection: An Ode" that "In our life alone does Nature live." For from his own experience, Wordsworth knew that Nature had actively affected him, and her role had to be taken into account.[10]

This belief in an active *and* passive mind has been called a paradox by Ernest de Selincourt, who characterized it further as "Hartley transcendentalized by Coleridge,"[11] in other words, as an incompatible combination of sensationalism (Hartley) and intuitionism (Coleridge) or of the mutually exclusive passive and active. But unlike Coleridge's paradox, which like all real paradoxes can be explained and ultimately makes sense, the "paradox" ascribed by de Selincourt to Wordsworth seems meant to describe an illogicality, perhaps even to suggest philosophical incompetence. For how can a mind be *both* active and passive?

Several scholars have claimed that Wordsworth simply changed from one view to the other,[12] but there seems to have been a fairly long period of transition in which both views ran concurrently; and even though Wordsworth, like Coleridge, continued to move in the direction of transcendental intuitionism, he never seems to have abandoned a belief in the active ministrations of nature.

There are also a number of explanations of how Wordsworth reconciled the contradiction. Melvin Rader posits a process of "ebb and flow," quoting an early Wordsworth verse fragment and commenting: "Wordsworth tried to understand 'the strange mystery' of this 'ebb and flow.' The human mind, he concluded, hearkens to 'voices of two different natures,' one of them received from sensory experience, the other from inmost modes of being."[13] Robert Langbaum, looking at the passage in *The Prelude* at the end of Book XII/XIII concerning "an ennobling interchange / Of action from without and from within," offers a more complicated explanation: "No two succeeding sensations from the same object can be the same, because the later sensation reaches a mind already modified by the earlier sensation," hence "the idea of interchange between man and nature—the idea that the mind modifies sensation as much as sensation modifies the mind." The mind, moreover, is itself part of the nature it perceives.[14]

Wordsworth at times is clearly struggling to work out his paradoxical view about the relationship of the mind to nature, of the inner to the outer, but one never senses that he would have abandoned the idea simply because he was unable to explain it theoretically. Wordsworth rather seems to have used a number of devices to accommodate the problematic relationship, for still other scholars have investigated a number of methods by which a blurring or blending of the mind and nature takes place in Wordsworth's poetry.

What is especially interesting and instructive is that these discoveries of techniques of blending came independently by very different methods and without, as it were, any deliberate intention; as far as I know, moreover, they have never been brought together. Only the last to appear, C.C.Clarke's *Romantic Paradox* (1962), is actually a study of the blending; Clarke notes Wordsworth's use of terms, such as "form" and "image," to refer to both objects and to their impressions on the mind, and he also notes the use of the same modifier applied to objects and to thoughts.[15]

The two other studies were earlier than Clarke's but are not mentioned by him. William Empson, writing about ten years earlier, noted a similar use by Wordsworth of the word "sense" to refer to both sensations and imagination united in a new faculty.[16] J.S.Lyon in his 1950 study of *The Excursion*, argues that Wordsworth developed a concept of "senses of the soul" that go well beyond the analogy of sense perception and spiritual intuition common in English poetry ("in the mind's eye") to a belief in the existence of "senses of the soul" linked with bodily senses, demonstrated by a fairly extensive and curious vocabulary for describing such things as "bodily eyes" and "inner eyes," found especially in *The Prelude* and *The Excursion*.[17] There is, I believe, no way of knowing for sure if all these devices were consciously created for the purpose of blending the inner and the outer or simply reflected Wordsworth's working view of things.

In the same vein, Mary Warnock, a professional philosopher who has recently studied the history of the imagination, brings a breath of freshening air into the study of Coleridge's and Wordsworth's philosophical views, which she claims are unprofessional; it is a mistake, she insists, to try to systematize them "with too much precision."[18] Wordsworth's views, philosophical, psychological, and otherwise, I would agree, are not the result of long bouts of theorizing and there are limits to systematizing them. Wordsworth saw the universe in a certain way and we are simply reassembling it; for Wordsworth, it was an experienced whole but we tend to break it down to analyze it, a natural and justifiable process, but also one we easily forget we have performed. A corollary is that very likely the largest cause of the difficulty of understanding Wordsworth's views in the first place is that he did not care to systematize them — or perhaps it is more accurate to say he was opposed to the divisions and distinctions required of a systematization that inevitably misrepresents things.

So it was with associationism, in which Wordsworth apparently found a reasonable explanation of the simpler workings of the mind in its most elemental operations. In the eighteenth century, associationism was connected for a while with empirical sensationalism, as providing the mechanism of the passive mind, by John Locke and his follower David Hartley. The next chapter will examine more closely this basic aspect of Wordsworth's psychology before going on to its wider manifestations.

NOTES

1. W. J. B. Owen and Jane W. Smyser, eds., *The Prose Works of William Wordsworth* (Oxford, 1974), II, 87.

2. *The Excursion*, IV, 946, 952–53, 961–64, 966–68.

3. Ernest de Selincourt, ed., *Journals of Dorothy Wordsworth* (New York, 1941), I, 398–99.

4. Ernest de Selincourt, ed., *The Letters of William and Dorothy Wordsworth: The Later Years, Part II*, second edition, revised by Alan G. Hill (Oxford, 1979), V, 455.

5. Hyder Rollins, ed., *The Letters of John Keats* (Cambridge, Mass., 1958), I, 387.

6. Rollins, I, 282.

7. A. B. Grosart, ed., *The Prose Works of William Wordsworth* (London, 1876), III, 487–88.

8. Jonathan Bishop, "Wordsworth and the 'Spots of Time,' " *English Literary History*, 26 (1959), 58.

9. Nicholas Brooke, "Coleridge's 'True and Original Realism,' " *Durham University Journal*, 5 (1961), 59.

10. Mary Warnock (*Imagination* [Berkeley, 1976], p. 126) is mistaken when she fails to distinguish, in two quotations, Coleridges's view of a totally active mind (". . . We receive but what we give") from Wordsworth's interchange of mind and nature (". . . Thou must give / Else never can receive"). Coleridge's quotation (which continues, "In thy life alone does nature live") does not allow for a "two-way relationship, the giving and receiving," as Wordsworth's does.

11. Ernest de Selincourt, ed., *William Wordsworth, The Prelude*, 2nd edition, rev. Helen Darbishire, (Oxford, 1959), p. lxix.

12. Alan Grob, *The Philosophic Mind: A Study of Wordsworth's Poetry and Thought 1797–1805*, (Columbus, 1973), p. 5, *passim*. Jonathan Wordsworth, *William Wordsworth: The Borders of Vision* (Oxford, 1982), pp. 338, 356.

13. Melvin Rader, *Wordsworth, A Philosophical Approach*, (Oxford, 1967), 119. The last two phrases quoted by Rader are from "Yes, it was the mountain Echo."

14. Robert Langbaum, *The Mysteries of Identity* (New York, 1977), p. 31.

15. C. C. Clarke, *Romantic Paradox: An Essay on the Poetry of Wordsworth* (London, 1962), pp. 25, 45.

16. William Empson, *The Structure of Complex Words* (London, 1977), p. 298.
17. J. S. Lyon, *The Excursion: A Study* (New Haven, 1950), pp. 96–104.
18. Warnock, p. 108.

II

Wordsworth and Eighteenth-Century Psychology

Despite his aversion to system, Wordsworth was not hesitant to accept a theoretical structure if it seemed to conform to his experience and to explain it satisfactorily. Such was the case with associationism, a psychological theory popular in the eighteenth century that appears in passages of his early works, notably in the Preface to *Lyrical Ballads* (1800) and in *The Prelude* (1799).

Several key passages of the Preface will be discussed below; an example from *The Prelude* occurs in Part I of *The Two-Part Prelude of 1799* (lines 417–443):

> The Earth
> And common face of Nature spake to me
> Rememberable things—sometimes, 'tis true,
> By quaint associations, yet not vain
> Nor profitless, if haply they impressed

Collateral objects and appearances,
Albeit lifeless then, and doomed to sleep
Until maturer seasons called them forth
To impregnate and to elevate the mind.
And if the vulgar joy by its own weight
Wearied itself out of the memory,
The scenes which were a witness of that joy
Remained, in their substantial lineaments
Depicted on the brain, and to the eye
Were visible, a daily sight. And thus
By the impressive agency of fear,
By pleasure and repeated happiness—
So frequently repeated—and by force
Of obscure feelings representative
Of joys that were forgotten, these same scenes,
So beauteous and majestic in themselves,
Though yet the day was distant, did at length
Become habitually dear, and all
Their hues and forms were by invisible links
Allied to the affections.

Wordsworth in this passage is trying to explain why he felt joys as a child that seemed to have no source. In preceding lines (399–412), he had remarked how as a ten-year-old he had been moved by seascapes he had not remembered witnessing before ("linking with the spectacle / No body of associated forms"). So, in the lines quoted above, he tells us that many of his early experiences of nature were seemingly forgotten, yet "associations" from nature "impressed" on his mind not only "rememberable things" but accompanying ("collateral") "objects and appearances," constituting whole scenes that "remained, in their substantial lineaments / Depicted on the brain . . ." and that were reinforced by daily view of them, as well as by feelings such as fear and happiness (presumably associated with them), until those scenes were "by invisible links / Allied to the affections."

The passage is somewhat difficult to follow, probably because the idea itself is complex, for associationist jargon is minimal. Yet the underlying ideas are characteristically associationist, both the unconscious operation of the mind in the associationist process and the linking of feelings with experiences and ideas, as well as the linking of various objects experienced in close conjunction temporally or spatially. Wordsworth, however, was not a true associationist, for even during the period in which he used associationist principles to explain phenomena, he didn't accept associationism as a fundamental, all-encompassing theory, and as he became more transcendentalist he had even less reason, as we shall see, to be an associationist.[1] On the other hand, his use of associationism is important, for it shows Wordsworth at his most derivative, and his connections with the system have long been confused to the point of interfering with a true estimate of his originality.

One eighteenth-century associationist is alleged to be a major influence on Wordsworth's psychology, David Hartley (1705–1757), an English physician, who published his *Observations on Man* in 1749. The hard facts in this matter are few and far between; Hartley is mentioned once by Wordsworth in a letter (1808) as among the "men of real power, who go before their age."[2] Without further external evidence, scholars have resorted to finding more and more traces of Hartley's psychological and philosophical theories in Wordsworth's poetry and criticism itself, until today Hartley's influence is widely accepted.[3]

To describe Hartley's psychology requires at least brief background information, for his was an associationist system and association psychology had been around for some time.[4] Aristotle concerned himself with laws of association based on similarity, contrast, and contiguity, but he didn't pursue the matter in great detail. English Associationist psychology was the next step; it grew directly out of the Empirical philosophy of Thomas Hobbes and John Locke, for if most knowledge comes to us through the senses, as Locke and Hobbes agreed, then there was need of some explanation how complex ideas could derive from simple sense perceptions.[5] The main counter-psychology was the so-called "nativist," such as the Scottish Intuitionists and, later, Kant, who offered an *a priori* system.

Generally ignored in this regard in the eighteenth century, Thomas Hobbes was nevertheless the first to deal with the association of ideas, even though he didn't use the term. He was especially concerned with memory and saw association as a natural movement of ideas. John Locke, on the other hand, was the first to use the term "association of ideas" (*Essay Concerning Human Understanding*, 4th ed.[1700]) but saw the process in a negative light: habit tended to connect ideas in the teeth of reason.

After the pioneering work of Hobbes and Locke, the associationist tradition divided into two loosely connected groups, one English, the other Scottish.[6] David Hume, the Scottish philosopher, followed Hobbes in seeing association as natural, although he considered himself original in this regard. Lord Kames, Alexander Gerard, and James Beattie followed Hume in this central belief of the naturalness of the association of ideas.

The English tradition beginning with John Locke

was provided its central tenets by David Hartley. Locke, whom Hartley claimed as his forebear, saw the mind as predominantly passive, even though Locke's "ideas of reflection" afforded at least a slightly active role to the mind. Hartley negated reflection, found the mind *totally* passive, and made the association of ideas the *only* explanation of complex mental phenomena. The method of association, moreover, was limited by Hartley to contiguity in time, but his theory set out to explain *all* human experience. Hartley was not the only associationist in eighteenth-century England, as seems so often to be assumed; he was simply the most radical and perhaps therefore the most famous.

As a strict empiricist, Hartley accepted only sensations and the "ideas" derived from sensations. The rest of his basic psychology is a matter of evolution from lower to higher forms:

> Any Sensations, A, B, C, etc. by being associated with one another a sufficient Number of Times, get such a Power over the corresponding Ideas, a, b, c, etc. that any one of the Sensations A, when impressed alone, shall be able to excite in the Mind b, c, etc. the Ideas of the rest.[7]

But such an evolution can take you only so far; a further mechanism was necessary to explain psychological phenomena beyond mere build-up of ideas. John Gay (1699–1745), a cousin of the poet of the same name and another source named by Hartley, provided the missing machinery in an esoteric manner. In an anonymous preface to a book by a minor philosopher published in 1731, Gay claimed that pleasure and pain are connected through association of ideas with actions and motives.[8] It is just these pleasures and pains that Hartley uses to explain the build-up of six classes of "intellectual affections" in six steps: imagination, ambition, self-interest, sympathy, theopathy, and (a sum of them all and, indeed, of each person) the moral sense. Each class of pleasures and pains coalesces with previous ones to form the next class. At this point we have arrived at advanced psychology.

The division between the Scottish and English traditions is valid but inexact. It is true that Hartley was followed in England by Joseph Priestley, who produced an abridgment of Hartley's *Observations* in 1775, and by William Godwin; but earlier in the century Joseph Addison, like Hume and his Scottish disciples, tended toward Hobbesian views. On the other hand, one Scot, Francis Hutcheson, fell in with more Lockean views, and another, Archibald Alison, fell between the two schools of thought. In any event, the mention of Godwin, a political philosopher, and Archibald Alison, a noted esthetician of the late eighteenth century, suggests the extent of the spread of associationist ideas into other fields. Even poetry began to reflect associationism, as evidenced by passages in Mark Akenside's *The Pleasures of Imagination*, Samuel Roger's *Pleasures of Memory*, and Erasmus Darwin's *Zoonomia*.

This brief history of the associationist theory current before William Wordsworth's career was well under way is meant to suggest just how pervasive such theory was by the end of the century. Howard C. Warren, the historian of associationist psychology, compares it in its pervasiveness with evolutionary theory late in the next century.[9] It is perhaps more to our point to compare late eighteenth-century associationism with late twentieth-century Freudian-Jungian psychology: it is found on everyone's lips, even of those who know little or nothing of Freud and Jung. An important difference, however, is that in this latter case the ideas are more easily traced to their specific sources, whereas there need be no one source for the popular associationist psychology of the late eighteenth century. "Hartleyan" does not equate with "associationist."[10]

If true, if associationism assumed the popular proportions it seems to have, the influence of David Hartley on William Wordsworth is considerably more difficult to trace than scholars have been aware in the absence of external evidence. For although Hartley was an important figure in the history of associationist psychology, he was not the only eighteenth-century figure involved, as we have already seen, nor, in view of the popular nature of the ideas, was Wordsworth's associationism necessarily traceable to direct sources.

At its most general, associationism is epistemological in nature; indeed, psychological theory before the nineteenth century is quite often a form of epistemology since the science of knowing is so involved in the psychological working of the mind. And, as we saw in Chapter I, the question for Wordsworth narrows down to whether the mind is passive (sensationalist) or active (transcendental). Locke had purposely rejected Descartes' theory of innate ideas, but Locke's sensationalist epistemology allowed for some mental activity in his "ideas of reflection." Just as purposely, Hartley rejected Locke's "ideas of reflection": ". . . All the most complex Ideas arise from Sensation; and . . . Reflection is not a distinct Source, as Mr. *Locke* makes it" (I, 360).[11] And yet, as Alan Grob has pointed out, the mind can never be seen as totally passive; even Hartley must leave room for some choice in perception and recollection.[12]

In any case, Grob also argues persuasively for a movement in Wordsworth's career away from sensationalism (at the root of eighteenth-century associationism) toward transcendentalism. However, Grob's tentative dates for the phases of the movement (1797–1800, 1802–1805; after 1805) tend to make the transitions seem too abrupt, despite his constant references to overlapping. For Wordsworth did manage to believe for a while in both sensationalism *and* transcendentalism, with mind both active *and* passive.

But if Wordsworth was more than a sensationalist, were his sensationalist beliefs at least derived from Hartley? ". . . Almost all of the general tenets of the sensationalist theory set forth by Hartley, could," according to Grob, "with very little modification, be subscribed to by Wordsworth," and yet, one might add, by most others of the time as well.[13] For, as Grob also points out, the view of the passive mind that directly derives from sensationalist theory was one of "the age's profoundest beliefs."[14] There are, moreover, other matters to consider before laying Wordsworth's epistemology (or at least half of it) at Hartley's door. Sense experience, for one thing, actually plays a small part in Hartley's theory, even though it is a *sine qua non* of associationism, whereas for Wordsworth sense experience itself was always a central interest. Likewise, Hartley considers the end of the long evolution of a sense experience to be "the moral sense"—removed as far as possible from the sense experience itself that Wordsworth so valued.[15] Such considerations do not make one comfortable with the idea of Hartley's profound influence on Wordsworth.

In the same way, when considering Hartley's possible influence on Wordsworth's literary theory, we are

confronted by Hartley's wholesale disparagement of the
liberal arts, including poetry.[16] The evidence in fact
doesn't seem to support any direct or significant Hartleyan influence on Wordsworth's literary theory. As
Martin Kallich observes: "Certainly, Hartley's conclusions about the nature of the pleasures of imagination
and about standards of taste must have had little influence upon Wordsworth, Coleridge, and the others,"
even though, Kallich assumes that, Hartley probably in-
directly influenced Wordsworth's psychological views.[17]

There are clearly associationist concepts in Wordsworth's theory, but whether they are derived from
Hartley's *Observations* is another, more difficult matter.
Some of what is often identified as Hartleyan consists
merely of Wordsworth's ambiguous use of terminology.
Sometimes influence is demonstrated by the mere use
by Wordsworth of the term *associate* and its cognates in
their normal, everyday denotation: "I am sensible that
my associations must have sometimes been particular
instead of general . . ." (I, 153), where "associations"
means simply "those arbitrary connections of feelings
and ideas with particular words and phrases," a common enough usage.

But beyond these misleading examples, there are the
inescapably associationist passages, possibly Hartleyan
in influence. The Preface to *Lyrical Ballads* (1800) contains the best instances:

> The principal object then which I proposed to
> myself in these Poems was to make the incidents
> of common life interesting by tracing in them,
> truly though not ostentatiously, the primary
> laws of our nature: chiefly as far as regards the

manner in which we associate ideas in a state of excitement. (I, 122, 124)

★　★　★

For our continued influxes of feeling are modified and directed by our thoughts, which are indeed the representatives of all our past feelings; and as by contemplating the relation of these general representatives to each other, we discover what is really important to men, so by the repetition and continuance of this act feelings connected with important subjects will be nourished, till at length, if we be originally possessed of much organic sensibility, such habits of mind will be produced that by obeying blindly and mechanically the impulses of those habits we shall describe objects and utter sentiments of such a nature and in such connection with each other, that the understanding of the being to whom we address ourselves, if he be in a healthful state of association, must necessarily be in some degree enlightened, his taste exalted, and his affections ameliorated. (I, 126)

It is difficult to disprove a case of specific influence, but it is well nigh impossible to disprove one where the evidence is offered as self-evident. In any event, neither of these passages has been *shown* to be heavily influenced by Hartley even though their associationist drift is unmistakable.

To approach, for a moment, from the other direction: there are a number of things that Hartley says about poetry in Proposition 94 (Book I) of his *Observations* that Wordsworth would surely have disagreed with.

It is true that both men did agree about the mimetic and universal aspects of poetry, as well as the concept of uniformity and variety (Wordsworth called it "similitude and dissimilitude") that explained such things as the pleasure afforded by meter.[18] These concepts were, however, commonplace in the eighteenth century.[19] On the other hand, Hartley defends "high-strained Expressions" on the ground of poetic license and also argued that it was necessary for the poet to "choose such Scenes as are beautiful, terrible, or otherwise strongly affecting" (I, 430, 431), whereas Wordsworth had no use at all for poeticisms and, as we have already seen, believed that feeling should give "importance to the action and situation and not the action and situation to the feeling" (I, 128). In such a view the scene (or "action and situation") are relatively unimportant. But, of course, Wordsworth did not have to accept Hartley's theory whole hog, and such disagreements do not preclude influence.

Turning from prose theory to poetic practice, we find the question of Hartleyan influence again problematic. For, considering the pervasiveness of associationist theory, we must find specific Hartleyan concepts in Wordsworth's poems or verbatim echoes in his diction to make anything like a firm case, and such evidence is hard to come by. Not that scholars haven't made some far-reaching claims that Wordsworth's poetry shows he had been reading his Hartley, or at least talking to Coleridge or Godwin, who had been reading *their* Hartley.[20]

Influence of ideas for the moment aside, there have never been any distinct verbal echoes of Hartley found in Wordsworth's works, at least as far as I am aware. The absence is unusual, for Wordsworth had a keen verbal memory and his poems resound with echoes of others' prose and verse, both those deliberately included by

Wordsworth and annotated by him and the many more he was apparently unaware of.

Further: Hartley's *Observations* is not a mere compendium of psychological generalizations; there are a large number of subordinate insights and comments that one might expect to show up in the works of a poet who was both occupied himself with psychological speculations and allegedly reading a work like the *Observations*. There are, as we have seen, occasional ideas in Hartley that occur in similar form in Wordsworth, but never so similar as to offer compelling evidence of influence. And if Wordsworth used distinctly Hartleyan ideas in his work, surely he would have been aware of them at least occasionally and would have given Hartley credit where due.

If there is no compelling reason to suspect Hartley of direct influence, were there at least other possible influences on Wordsworth's associationist ideas, especially any that might be more compatible with his idea of a mind that is active as well as passive?

We know that Hartley's reputation was rising towards the end of the eighteenth century. As already mentioned, Joseph Priestley published an abridgement of the *Observations* in 1775. And two influences on Wordsworth's thinking in the 1790's, William Godwin and Samuel Taylor Coleridge, both themselves subscribed to Hartleyan views, including the idea of a passive mind. Godwin, of course, was a major political theorist of the time, having published his *Enquiry Concerning Political Justice* in 1793. Coleridge, on the other hand, was not yet well known, but was so taken with Hartley's ideas that he named his first son Hartley Coleridge. From what is known only of Wordsworth and his acquaintances one might therefore suppose Hartley's views prominent and influential enough to require some effort at the time to circumvent.

It might seem surprising, then, that Wordsworth could so effortlessly disregard Hartley's central theory of mental passivity in "Tintern Abbey" (1798):

> Therefore am I still
> A lover of the meadows and the woods,
> And mountains; and of all that we behold
> From this green earth; of all the mighty world
> Of eye, and ear, —both what they half create,
> And what perceive. . . .
> (lines 102–107)

Or in this passage from the earliest version of the *Prelude* (1798–99), where man is described as:

> An inmate of this *active* universe;
> From nature largely he receives, nor so
> Is satisfied but largely gives again,
> For feeling has to him imparted strength,
> And powerful in all sentiments of grief,
> Of exultation, fear and joy, his mind,
> Even as an agent of the one great mind,
> Creates, creator and receiver both. . . .[21]

This combination of an active and a passive mind Ernest de Selincourt describes as witnessing an epistemological paradox—"Hartley transcendentalized by Coleridge."[22] But there is, I believe, a further explanation that allows Wordsworth more independence and makes him still more of a man of his times than Coleridge.

For what is not common knowledge is just how early the English reaction against Hartley set in. Some later rejections are well known: Coleridge devoted three full chapters of his *Biographia Literaria* (1817) to demolishing Hartley's theories. William Hazlitt, moreover, another Wordsworth acquaintance and still a relatively unknown literary figure at the time, published an anonymous attack on Hartley's system in 1805.[23] But the reaction had already set in solidly by the early 1790's in the work of Abraham Tucker, Archibald Alison, and Dugald Stewart. By 1798, such passages from Wordsworth's poetry as those in question were less revolutionary than they might seem. Not only was associationism in the air, but anti-Hartleyan sentiment was coming into its own as well.

All three of those mentioned were associationists, and all three published works well before Coleridge had changed his mind about Hartley in the early 1800's.[24] Abraham Tucker's *Light of Nature Pursued* appeared in 1768, that is, between Hartley's original edition of *Observations* (1749) and Priestley's abridgment in 1775. (An abridgment of Tucker's work, it is worth noting, was itself published by William Hazlitt in 1807).[25] Associationist psychology was part of Tucker's theory of mind, but it was not central and all-inclusive as it was with Hartley.

Archibald Alison's *Essays on the Nature and Principles of Taste* (1790) resulted perhaps partly from a remark by Tucker: "A third source of beauty is translation [association]: whatever has been the occasion of much or frequent delight becomes agreeable in our eye[,] satisfaction being transferred from the effects to the cause."[26] In any case, Alison was an esthetician who founded his theory largely on association of ideas, although a good deal of his theory was based as well on concepts of unity and decorum, which seem to have little or no connection with associationism.

Dugald Stewart, who published his *Elements of the Philosophy of the Human Mind* in 1792, was more clearly a psychological theorist than the others, but, even though he devoted a long chapter to the association of ideas, he was less centrally an associationist than Alison. At least he was not so technically nor theoretically interested in associationism, being much more common-sensical and concerned with practical applications. Such an approach might well have appealed to William Wordsworth.

All three of these associationists believed in the activity of the mind, two of them openly objecting to Hartley on the issue. Abraham Tucker rejected the Hartleyan idea that the mind "sits a spectator only and not an agent of all we perform; [that] she may indeed discern what is doing but has no share in what is done . . ." (I, i, 50). On the contrary, he argued, we may "ascribe our actions to the performance of the mind because it depends entirely upon her of what kind that shall be" (I, i, 63).[27]

Archibald Alison is least clear on the matter of whether the mind is partly active or altogether passive; he never addresses the issue at all; but there is some evidence that he, like Wordsworth, thought it was both active and passive. His emphasis nevertheless is on a passive association of things we consider sublime or beautiful with other things that give us pleasure. But Alison escapes the relativism inherent in such frequently subjective associations by occasionally assuming that the mind actively discerns something sublime or beautiful actually existing in things themselves. Or at least such seems to be the implication of certain remarks:

> To reduce the great variety of instances of Beauty
> in Forms to any single principle, seems at first
> sight altogether impossible; not only from this
> variety, but also, in innumerable cases, from the
> contrary nature of the Forms, *which, in fact, are
> Beautiful.*[28]

If beauty is *inherent* in certain forms then it is no longer
dependent on a mind passively making associations. If
beauty is not merely the result of associations, it follows
further, it must be discovered by an active mind. Not
only are comments like the above sprinkled about his
work, but Alison generally seems to assume that his
judgments concerning what is sublime and beautiful are
valid in an absolute way that precludes simple association.

Dugald Stewart was closer to Abraham Tucker in his
clear rejection of Hartley's theory of the passive mind.
To begin with, Stewart described the mind early on in
his *Elements* as an "active principle."[29] All ideas, he explained later (I, 100–102), derive ultimately from sense
perceptions, but much of the mind would work in their
absence anyway. As for Hartley specifically, Stewart
hasn't much good to say. Even "our habitual actions
may be voluntary," for all that Hartley proved to the
contrary (I, 111, 297); likewise, the mind seems even to
be able to control the train of thoughts involved in associationism (I, 334). And in a more general way, Stewart argued further, "there must be some limit, beyond
which the theory of association cannot possibly be carried; for the explanation which it gives, of the formation
of new principles of action, proceeds on the supposition
that there are other principles previously existing in the
mind. The great question then is, when we are arrived

at this limit; or, in other words, when we are arrived at
the simple and original laws of our constitution" (I,
391). While others have multiplied such principles beyond belief, Hartley has surely been too eager to narrow
them.

Hartley and his followers may think he stops too
short, but, Stewart argues, *they* have gone too far too
fast, eschewing scientific method for *a priori* speculations:

> . . . In all the other sciences, the progress of dis-
> covery has been gradual, from the less general to
> the more general laws of nature; and . . . it would
> be singular, indeed, if, in the Philosophy of the
> Human Mind, a science, which but a few years
> ago was confessedly in its infancy, and which
> certainly labours under many disadvantages pe-
> culiar to itself, a step should, all at once, be made
> to a single principle comprehending all the par-
> ticular phenomena which we know (I, 398).[30]

Hartley's *a priori* reduction of all psychology to association by contiguity is what Stewart is objecting to.

Just this empirical bent of Stewart may well have
been a further attraction to Wordsworth, were there
need of one, and it is a virtue shared by all three of the
philosophers in question. Tucker, like Stewart and Alison, rarely strays far from experience, citing examples
constantly; "the abstract," as Tucker puts it, "is seen
clearest in the concrete" (I, i, 149). Dugald Stewart went
beyond the others, and beyond Wordsworth as well, in
espousing nominalist views that deny any sort of existence to universals (I, 190).[31]

Dugald Stewart, in any event, offers the most potential for having influenced William Wordsworth's psychological theories. Stewart's *Elements*, which ran through six editions by 1818, was the least complicated, most empirical of the three revisionists of Hartley. He laced his theorizing, moreover, with the sort of moral and religious speculation that might well have appealed to Wordsworth.

But of the three philosophers presented as alternatives to Hartley, only the work of Abraham Tucker was contained in Wordsworth's library at Rydal Mount (as was Hartley's *Observations* as well).[32] Even so, there is no external evidence that Wordsworth had read all or any one of the three, just as there is no evidence that he had read Hartley. All three figures, however, had substantial enough reputations to have come to Wordsworth's notice, and for the most part their views were compatible with his.

But the point of this chapter is not to refute Hartley's influence on Wordsworth; thorough refutation of course is impossible in any event. My aim is more modest—to convey with some force that that influence was not necessary. That Hartleyan influence has also not been proven is, I believe, worth repeating here as well; the history of Hartley-Wordsworth scholarship seems rather to support the truth of one of Tucker's contentions: "A bare assertion frequently reiterated may supply the place of evidence: scarce anybody but has found occasion to remark how the tenets of a sect or party continually chimed in men's ears without any argument to support them, have been at length received as articles of faith . . ." (I, i, 289–90).

It would compound the problem to insist that one or all of the three figures I have brought forward was an influence on Wordsworth, and I have no intention of doing so. But if no other end is served by examining the possibility, it is enough for my purpose if it suggests how pervasive some of Wordsworth's psychological ideas were at the time, thus setting the Hartleyan possibility in clearer perspective. And at the very least Tucker, Alison, and Stewart could have provided the young Wordsworth with examples of independent spirits, who, although they (like Hartley) were associationists, were also capable of believing (like Wordsworth) in a mind that was also active.

For some reason, William Wordsworth is often portrayed as a thinker more or less at the mercy of more powerful minds, especially that of Samuel Taylor Coleridge. With a normal susceptibility to the influence of others' ideas, Wordsworth, I suspect, was a more independent and original thinker than he is often given credit for. In this instance, the influence of Coleridge seems to have been exaggerated and that of Hartley almost certainly so.

NOTES

1. Howard C.Warren, *A History of the Association Psychology* (New York, 1921), pp. 9–10.
2. William Wordsworth to Richard Sharp (September 27, 1808), *The Letters of William and Dorothy Wordsworth*, arranged and edited by Ernest de Selincourt, 2nd ed., revised by Mary Moorman, Vol. II, *The Middle Years, Part I, 1806–1811* (Oxford, 1969), 266. Hartley's *Observations on Man*, however, is called "Hartley's book upon Man" and is merely used as an example of the slow development of the reputation of philosophers.
3. For a more detailed account of Hartley—Wordsworth scholarship, see John Hayden, "Wordsworth, Hartley, and the Revisionists," *Studies in Philology* 81 (1984), 94–118.
4. The best single work on the subject is still Howard C.Warren's

A History of the Association Psychology from Hartley to Lewis (New York, 1921).

5. Warren, p. 10.

6. This division is implicit in Martin Kallich, *The Association of Ideas and Critical Theory in Eighteenth-Century England* (The Hague, 1970).

7. David Hartley, *Observations on Man* (1749), I, 65, fac. ed. Garland Publishing Co. (New York, 1971) (all future citations will appear in the text). For a clear expansion of this principle see Warren, pp. 53–55.

8. "Dissertation on the Fundamental Principle of Virtue," preface to William King, *Origin of Evil*, trans. Edmund Law (1731).

9. Warren, p. 160. See also Kallich, pp. 16, 71, 267–70.

10. See Kallich, p. 131n: ". . . Beatty draws an elaborate parallel between the views of Hartley and Wordsworth and infers that Hartley is the chief and probably the only influence upon Wordsworth's associationism. In the light of current knowledge concerning the associationist climate of opinion at the turn of the century, such an inference is entirely unwarranted." Kallich does, nevertheless, seem to assume that Hartley was a major influence on Wordsworth; see, for example, p. 131.

11. Hartley adds (I, 360–61): ". . . It is, however, of little Consequence. We may conceive, that he called such Ideas as he could analyse up to Sensation, Ideas of Sensation; the rest Ideas of Reflection, using Reflection as a Term of Art, denoting an unknown Quantity. Besides which it may be remarked, that the Words which, according to him, stand for Ideas of Reflection, are, in general, Words, that, according to the Theory of these Papers, have no Ideas, but Definitions only. . . . If these Words have no immediate Ideas, there will be no Occasion to have recourse to Reflection as a source of Ideas; and, upon the Whole, there is no material Repugnancy between the Consequences of this Theory, and any thing advanced by Mr. *Locke*."

12. Alan Grob, *The Philosophic Mind* (Columbus, Ohio, 1973), pp. 59–60.

13. Grob, p. 137.

14. Grob, p. 60.

15. Toshikazu Maekawa, "Wordsworth and David Hartley's Philosophy," *Studies in Literature* (Fukuoka, Japan) 2 (1959), 157 [in Japanese].

16. ". . . It is evident, that most Kinds of Music, Painting, and Poetry,

have close connexions with Vice, particularly with the Vices of Intemperance and Lewdness; that they represent them in gay, pleasing colours, or, at least, take off from the Abhorrence due to them; that they cannot be enjoyed without *evilCommunications*, and Concurrence in the Pagan Show and Pomp of the World; and that they introduce a Frame of Mind, quite opposite to that of Devotion, and earnest Concern for our own and others future Welfare. This is evident of public Diversions, Collections of Pictures, Academies for Painting, Statuary, &c. ancient heathen Poetry, modern Poetry of most Kinds, Plays, Romances, &c. If there by any who doubt of this, it must be from the Want of a duly serious Frame of Mind," Hartley, II, 253–54. Hartley does, however, qualify the above stricture: ". . . All these Arts are capable of being devoted to the immediate Service of God and Religion in an eminent manner; and, when so devoted, they not only improve and exalt the Mind, but are themselves improved and exalted to a much higher Degree, than when employed upon profane Subjects. . . ." and yet, ". . . Upon the whole, it will follow, that the polite Arts are scarce to be allowed, except when consecrated to religious Purposes . . ." (II, 254).

17. Kallich, p. 131. No proof is offered for the latter view.
18. Hartley, I, 419, 430, 431. For Wordsworth's views on mimesis and universality, see John Hayden, *Polestar of the Ancients* (Newark, 1979), pp. 172–74. For Wordsworth on similitude and dissimilitude, see Owen and Smyser, I, 149.
19. Kallich, p.124.
20. For evaluation of specific claims, see Hayden, "Wordsworth, Hartley," pp. 105–108.
21. William Wordsworth, *The Prelude, 1798–1799*, ed. Stephen Parrish (Ithaca, NY, 1977), pp. 61–62.
22. Ernest de Selincourt, ed. *William Wordsworth: The Prelude* (Oxford, 1959), p. lxix.
23. "Remarks on the Systems of Hartley and Helvetius," appended to *An Essay on the Principles of Human Action*, in *The Complete Works of William Hazlitt*, ed. P. P. Howe (London, 1930), I, 50–91.
24. For Coleridge's change of philosophy, see E. K. Chambers, *Samuel Taylor Coleridge: A Biographical Study* (Oxford, 1938), p. 139.
25. *An Abridgement of the Light of Nature Pursued* (London, 1807). This anonymous abridgment contained a preface and Introduction by Hazlitt. Coleridge also was to write a preface to this abridgment of Tucker (attacking Hartley); see Chambers, p. 171.

26. Tucker, I, ii, 107. All future citations of this edition will appear in the text.

27. See also I, i, 67–77; II, i, 95–96.

28. Archibald Alison, *Essays on the Nature and Principles of Taste* (1790), facs. ed., Georg Olms Verlagsbuchhandlung (Hildesheim, 1968), pp.222–23 (italics added). At one point in the Conclusion, Alison states "that Matter *is not beautiful in itself*, without reference to Mind; and that its Beauty arises from the Expressions which an intelligent Mind connects with, *and perceives in it* . . ." (p. 411, italics added).

29. Dugald Stewart, *Elements of the Philosophy of the Human Mind* (London, 1818), I, 63. All future citations to this edition will appear in the text.

30. See also Thomas Reid, *Essays on the Intellectual Powers of Man* (Edinburgh, 1785), pp. 85–94, for an attack on Hartley's unscientific method by Stewart's mentor.

31. For more specific instances of possible influence of the three on Wordsworth, see John Hayden, "Wordsworth, Hartley," pp. 113–117.

32. Chester L.Shaver and Alice C.Shaver, *Wordsworth's Library: A Catalogue* (New York, 1979), pp. 333, 352. Both books were listed as borrowed from Coleridge.

Wordsworth and Observational Psychology

William Wordsworth was interested in a psychology based on observation rather than on experiment. For, in a real sense, the environments in which he was placed, especially the Lake District, were his laboratories, where in an unstructured fashion he could scrutinize his own mind and those of his contemporaries. In *The Prelude*, he put it plainly:

> When I began to inquire,
> To watch and question those I met, and held
> Familiar talk with them, the lonely roads
> Were schools to me in which I daily read
> With most delight the passions of mankind,
> There saw into the depth of human souls—
> Souls that appear to have no depth at all
> To vulgar eyes.
>
> (1805; XII, 161–68)

With such a passage in mind, it does not seem odd to speak even of Wordworth's "clinical" psychology, and the phrase, moreover, is useful as a reminder of the kind of psychology Wordsworth was engaged with, especially since, as we shall see, it is sometimes suggested that he was involved in experimental psychology with its case-study method.

Another helpful caveat at this point concerns the connotation of the word *psychology*, for to most people *psychology* means *abnormal psychology*. Indeed, a recent study by James Averill views Wordsworth's psychology in just that way; to Averill *Lyrical Ballads* are primarily "experiments in psychology" that reflect Wordsworth's love of suffering and his influence by the eighteenth-century sentimental tradition.[1] The case for influence is very convincing; many of the early poems, such as "Salisbury Plain," *An Evening Walk*, and some of *Lyrical Ballads* ("Her Eyes Are Wild" and "Complaint of the Forsaken Indian Woman"), do exhibit an unhealthy sentimental interest in suffering and in abnormal psychology itself.

But, as is not uncommon when a strong case is being made, Averill overstates it. Not only, in his view, is Wordsworth's poetry "inevitably the poetry of suffering" even up to the composition of *The White Doe of Rylstone* (1808), but Averill also claims that "through his poetry, after all, troops a veritable parade of victims; the insane, the miserable, the diseased, decrepit, dying, and dead populate his landscape *to the virtual exclusion of the healthy and the normal*" (italics added).[2] I would like to argue on the contrary that except for some of the early poems, Wordsworth was much more interested as a poet in the healthy and the normal and that early in his career he had all but left an interest in abnormal psychology behind, as well as the sort of mental or emotional bias that is interested in human suffering for its own sake. There is an exact emotional rightness, I would further argue, in the theme and tone of such poems about human suffering as "The Last of the Flock," "Simon Lee," and "The Old Cumberland Beggar," all written in 1798.

On the other side, there is a lingering attitude today that Wordsworth was a kind of cold fish in his works and in his life: the writer of the blurb on the dust-jacket of the recent edition of his lost letters to his wife claims that the letters show him as "indeed more human." At least it is easier to answer this charge of lack of emotion and involvement: anyone who could write "Resolution and Independence" or "Elegiac Stanzas" is surely as human as anyone could reasonably wish.

Be that as it may, Donald Davie long ago pointed out that Wordsworth was primarily interested in healthy states of mind—a position diametrically opposed to Averill's and, I believe, closer to the truth of the matter.[3] And so we have in Wordsworth the somewhat unusual interest in normal, healthy psychology—he was searching for what makes a mind well. In other words, what he was interested in principally was what he wished for Coleridge in *The Two-Part Prelude of 1799*: "health and the quiet of a healthful mind" (Second Part, line 510). And, as we will see in the last chapter, Wordsworth was very concerned with the pre-eminently healthy state of joy. This emphasis on healthy states of mind and generally on *normal* psychology is, I believe, his most important and most ignored contribution as a poet.

Throughout his career, Wordsworth speculated about psychological phenomena. Few of his poems have no psychological element and many poems have little else, at least by way of theme. Again, the poet was quite aware of his preoccupation; in a letter of 1807 he is explicit: "There is scarcely one of my Poems which does not aim to direct the attention to some moral sentiment, or to some general principle, or law of thought, or of our intellectual constitution."[4] And in typically forthright fashion, Wordsworth claimed in conversation (1841) that his "writings were founded on what was true and spiritual in human nature" and would eventually be read and be thereby useful, especially to the young.[5]

With such a predisposition toward psychology but away from large psychological schematization, Wordsworth set forth his views on psychological development principally as reflected by one individual—himself as depicted in the semi-autobiographical *Prelude* and to a lesser extent in "Tintern Abbey" and "Ode: Intimations." Together or apart, none of these poems of course even nearly constitutes a treatise on the subject nor, being contained in poems, is the chronology of development always very clear. Indeed, Wordsworth was aware of the difficulties involved; "Hard task to analyze a soul," he insisted in the second Book of *The Prelude* (1805; ll.208–15) and commented:

> . . . Who shall parcel out
> His intellect by geometric rules,
> Split like a province into round and square?
> Who knows the individual hour in which
> His habits were first sown even as a seed,
> Who that shall point as with a wand, and say
> "This portion of the river of my mind
> Came from yon fountain?"

Not surprisingly, considering the place of the visionary in his own life, Wordsworth viewed the psychologi-

cal life in general as revolving around visionary capabilities of the sort whose absence is lamented so openly in
"Ode: Intimations." There are, to begin with, essentially three kinds of people: the common, the corrupted,
and the gifted. All three have the ability to see beyond
the visible world, at least in childhood, when the ability
is at its strongest.

The visionary ability is likewise lost by all three
kinds of people. The corrupted man loses his through
apathy or meanness—"little enmities and low desires"
(1805; II, 447)—or is "by sensible impressions . . . en-
thralled" (1805; XIII, 103). What Wordsworth called
"common minds" (1805; II, 405), like the gifted or
"higher minds" (XIII, 90) to a lesser extent, lose theirs
through the simple aging process, as their coping with
the everyday world makes more and more conflicting
demands ("Ode: Intimations," ll. 72–77). Even the
gifted do eventually lose the visionary power, at least in
part:

> . . . The hiding-places of my power
> Seem open, I approach, and then they close;
> I see by glimpses now, when age comes on
> May scarcely see at all. . . .
>
> (1805; XI, 335–38)

And yet all people have some visionary experience:
". . . There's not a man/That lives who hath not had his
god-like hours" (1805; III, 191–92).

Wordsworth's life, as regards this triple-layered visionary potential, is clearly a model of the gifted or
"higher" mind, but to some extent it exemplifies all
three. And while he does follow his development from
infancy to childhood, then to late adolescence, and fi-

nally to maturity, these stages are not clear-cut. Infancy, which is described in a well-known passage in Book II of *The Prelude* (1805; ll. 237–303), is the most generalized of the stages in man's psychological development, perhaps because Wordsworth had no memories of such early events in his own life and had to depend on observation and "conjectures" (l. 238). An infant, the lines tell us, "gathers" love from his mother's eyes and facial expressions, and this love allows his mind to be watchful and to form the first comprehensive wholes of experience; and thus the faculties—even the "poetic spirit" or visionary faculty—are nurtured. The underlying truth to the passage can be confirmed by reference to the arrested or stunted development of children who are raised as infants in institutions that provide insufficient affection.

The infant's mind, in any event, grows as more and more data are taken in and stored, and the bond with his mother becomes a bond with nature (1805; II, 237–64). By now, however, we are arrived at childhood, wherein "the foundations of [the] mind were laid" (*Excursion* I, 132). And while the description of human development becomes more personal, it also becomes more thorny: "Yet is a path/More difficult before me . . ." (1805; II, 287–88).

At this point, moreover, the child becomes more an example of the higher mind. The spots of time occur most conspicuously in childhood with their renovative power for later days, and children are "privileged to hold Divine communion" (*PW*, III, 57). But although Wordsworth's narrator is exemplary of the more gifted visionary, we can see from other poems, such as "Ode: Intimations," that childhood in general is a time for vision.

At other periods, however, the child in *The Prelude* yielded himself up to nature through pure sensual pleasure, his affections became connected with natural scenes, and nature enlarged his sympathies (1805; I, 586–93, 625–40; II, 181–93). Later, nature led to love of man (1805; VIII, 69–81).

By late adolescence, his communion with nature had deepened still further, and his feelings, steeped in nature, spread to all and he saw the One Life (1805; II, 371–77, 415–30). He looked for the universality of things, but he was still bound by the power of his eyes, and nature was still more important than man (1805; III, 106–20, 155–67; VIII, 864–68). Maturity brought him closest to the lot of the corrupted individual, for he probed into the meaning of things and despaired (1805; X, 878–900). His imaginative strength, however, overcame the despair and he became "a sensitive, and a *creative* soul" (1805; XI, 250–57). Through meditation and suffering, moreover, he avoids "cares and low pursuits" and habits that enslave the mind and turn the gifted into the corrupted (1805; XIII, 123–43). The visionary potential, nevertheless, that he had been more optimistic about earlier in *The Prelude* (1805; II, 275–80), seems to dissipate in maturity as we have already seen, and yet returns, we are told in *The Excursion* (IX, 63–64), in old age, when "the gross and visible frame of things/Relinquishes its hold upon the sense. . . ."

This psychological profile of human life is hardly complete, but on the whole *The Prelude* was probably not intended to present a general profile even though there are universal overtones, especially in the passage on infancy. The profile is also slanted in the direction of visionary activity and this side will be dealt with in more detail in the last chapter.

If Wordsworth wrote no treatise on psychological development, one might at least expect a good deal of in-depth characterization as the vehicle for psychological probing in a poet I have said to be almost obsessed with psychology. And yet Wordsworth wrote only one drama, no prose fiction, and few long narrative poems (as narrative poems). Even what there are of the usual genres involving characterization, moreover, are not used on the whole for psychological probing.

It was not that Wordsworth was uninterested in such use of characterization or was unaware of the potential. He realized, for example, the psychological complexity of Shakespeare's plays, perhaps more than most people. Writing of a boy-actor playing Hamlet, he exclaimed, referring to the youth's necessary inexperience: ". . . It is certainly impossible that he should understand the character, that is the composition of the character."[6] And yet, considering the paucity of characterization in his own poems, it is odd that he once wrote, "It seems to me, that in poems descriptive of human nature, however short they may be, character is absolutely necessary, &c.: incidents are among the lowest allurements of poetry."[7] From such a statement one might anticipate something different in Wordsworth's poetry than what one finds.

Wordsworth's awareness of the importance of characterization, nevertheless, did translate into realistic touches at times in some of his narrative poems. In "Michael" (Wordsworth wrote to Charles James Fox) he was attempting to display "the domestic affections," and much scholarship has been devoted to the relationship of Michael and Luke.[8] But there is another character in the poem, Isabel, Michael's wife, who is for my purposes more important, for Wordsworth took time from

the impressive but simple portrait of Michael to give
some realistic touches to her characterization. She dis-
plays "domestic affection" too, and it is her affection for
Luke that is so engaging. When she is first told of Michael's decision to send Luke away, she has to daydream
immediately of "Richard Bateman" as a way of soften-
ing the pain of separation, for he had likewise left the
parish for London and then had become a great success.
Two days later, Isabel has second thoughts when she observes the effects of the plans on Michael, and tells Luke
of her fears, whereupon (ll. 299–301)

> The Youth made answer with a jocund voice;
> And Isabel, when she had told her fears,
> Recovered heart.

Following the pattern already set by Michael after he
had told *her* of his decision and "to the fields went forth
/ With a light heart" (ll. 283–84), Isabel thus rids herself
of anxiety by expressing it. Later, the hope and pride
she felt in her daydream returns when the letter concerning Luke arrives; as she shows it off to her neighbors she
reminds one of Betty Foy in "The Idiot Boy," who was
also carried away by admiration for *her* son. Then the
complexity of Isabel is demonstrated by the return of
her reluctance to see Luke go as she attempts to delay
his departure (ll. 317–21):

>   To this word
> The Housewife answered, talking much of things
> Which, if at such short notice he should go,
> Would surely be forgotten. But at length
> She gave consent, and Michael was at ease.

Her vacillation between pride and anxiety is both charming and realistic.

Another instance of realistic characterization—this time in a set of poems called "The Matthew Poems"—seems to me to have been misunderstood as often as it has been interpreted. Matthew, in the poem of the same name, is represented as a walking paradox:

> The sighs which Matthew heaved were sighs
> Of one tired out with fun and madness;
> The tears which came to Matthew's eyes
> Were tears of light, the dew of gladness.

This portrait of the weeping clown is continued in the two companion poems, "The Two April Mornings" and "The Fountain."

In "The Two April Mornings," Matthew, described in the second stanza as "blithe," stops in the first stanza and says unaccountably, "The Will of God be done!"—not a statement one might expect a blithe man to utter. Later on in the poem we find that the statement was elicited by the similarity of the day with one thirty years before when, on visiting his nine-year-old daughter's grave, he was confronted by "a blooming girl." She seemed to him "a pure delight," and yet he says:

> "There came from me a sigh of pain
> Which I could ill confine;
> I looked at her, and looked again:
> And did not wish her mine!"

The narrator then remarks that Matthew is now dead and the narrator envisions him "with a bough / Of

wilding in his hand"—possibly part of the burial ritual
in the Lake District.[9]

Matthew's curious rejection of the "blooming girl,"
which is surely at the center of the poem's meaning, has
been variously interpreted, usually in a positive way.
The most valid of these in my opinion is David Ferry's:
Matthew's acceptance of the girl "would be taking up
again the burden of human relationships with their joy
and attendant sorrow. And he does not wish her his because the joy her living beauty offers him is as nothing
compared to the depth of his relationship to the dead."[10]
The beginning of Ferry's interpretation seems to me the
real point: Matthew does not wish to expose himself
again to the same pain he felt when he lost his daughter.
But no invidious comparison between the girl and his
daughter, suggested by the rest of Ferry's reading,
seems even implicit. Matthew is simply too sensitive to
cope with more pain—he cannot "confine" "a sigh of
pain."

Notice, however, that there is no comment whatever
by the narrator (or poet) that could be construed as a
criticism of Matthew's behavior, what might be seen as
(but isn't) a rejection of life. Like the shepherd in "The
Last of the Flock," Matthew suffers from his humanness
and is not to be looked down upon for it.

In "The Fountain," Matthew is described by the narrator as "The grey-haired man of glee" but again we see
behind the facade which apparently he has erected for
the public. To the narrator he makes the curious comment:

> "And yet the wiser mind
> Mourns less for what age takes away
> Than what it leaves behind."

In the context, what age takes away is clearly youth; what it has left behind in Matthew's case (and he seems to be universalizing his own experience) are memories and sorrow for his dead daughter—suggested by lines 49–52. Then, he compares birds in their innocence and freedom with man, adding the comment:

> "But we are pressed by heavy laws;
> And often, glad no more,
> We wear a face of joy, because
> We have been glad of yore."

Man, in Matthew's view, often merely pretends to be joyful (wears "a face of joy") despite suffering. Matthew, at least, seems to have resorted to such pretense, for later he calls himself (by implication) "the man of mirth" yet claims that despite a life well spent he is "by none . . . enough beloved," not enough apparently to compensate for the pain he has endured. He goes on to reject the narrator's offer to be a son to him, much as he had rejected the "blooming girl" in "The Two April Mornings," and then he begins to sing "witty rhymes." This portrait of the suffering sensitive man is once again unmarked by disapproval.

The paradoxical mixture of mirth and sadness—the mirth veiling the sadness—continues in several unpublished fragments that also concern Matthew, especially "Elegy Written in the Same Place" (*PW*, IV, 453):

> Remembering how thou didst beguile
> With thy w[ild] ways our eyes and ears,
> I feel more sorrow in a smile
> Than in a waggon-load of tears. . . .

And in "Address to the Scholars," the expression in the "Dirge" at Matthew's funeral, "sorrow overcharged with pain," while part of what it is hoped the mourners will avoid, is really an apt description of what Matthew had himself to endure.

One must turn to another later poem outside the Matthew series to find an instance similar to Matthew's reluctance to leave himself open to more grief after the death of his daughter. In "Maternal Grief," a boy avoids his mourning mother, who reminds him of the recent death of his twin sister:

> And full oft the Boy,
> Now first acquainted with distress and grief,
> Shrunk from his Mother's presence,
>   shunned with fear
> Her sad approach, and stole away to find,
> In his own haunts of joy where'er he might,
> A more congenial object.

With the boy, however, the reluctance to expose himself to "distress and grief" is mixed with fear of newly discovered death.

Such insightful strokes in the characterization of normal people occur frequently enough in Wordsworth's poems to show both his greater interest and capabilities in that direction. But, as we shall see, much more of Wordsworth's characterization (as distinguished from other forms of psychological probing) is devoted to abnormal psychology; perhaps, after all, characterization lends itself more readily to the abnormal—to the homicidal, to the nearly mad, to the stuff, that is, of tragedies.

A considerable part of Wordsworth's "normal psychology," in any case, took the form of statements, sometimes a summation of the theme of a poem but often simply an aside. In the sonnet "Those words were uttered as in pensive mood," the shapes of objects found in clouds are said not to appeal finally to man, and then there follows an explanation, the central point of the poem: "The immortal Mind craves objects that endure." Another sonnet "Bothwell Castle," is concluded by a similar provocative summation:

> Memory, like sleep, hath powers which
>   dreams obey,
> Dreams, vivid dreams, that are not fugitive:
> How little that she cherishes is lost!

For most of us, that is, memory tends to retain pleasant thoughts, especially as we grow older. Finally, in an aside in *The Prelude* (1805; XII, 197–201) that might be said to have influenced Keats (*Lamia*, Part II, 1–2) had he had access to it, we are told that where there is "labor in excess and poverty . . . there indeed / Love cannot be." The only difference between Keats and Wordsworth in conveying this insight is in the delivery, for Keats sounds sophomoric ("Love in a hut, with water and a crust, / Is—Love, forgive us!—cinders, ashes, dust. . . ."), while Wordsworth manages to remain dignified.

The main ingredients of these statements of psychological insight are morality and truth, both of which Wordsworth, I believe, possessed in abundance. Man, in his view, is essentially moral;[11] and all his actions are the result of habit we learn from the "Essay on Morals."[12] That morality depends on habit is also implicit in Wordsworth's view of the moral working of poetry set forth in the Preface to *Lyrical Ballads* (1800):

. . . if we be originally possessed of much organic sensibility, such habits of mind will be produced that by obeying blindly and mechanically the impulses of those habits we shall describe objects and utter sentiments of such a nature and in such connection with each other, that the understanding of the being to whom we address ourselves, if he be in a healthful state of association, must necessarily be in some degree enlightened, his taste exalted, and his affections ameliorated.[13]

This important pronouncement,[14] as well as the entire view of morality as habitual, can in fact be seen as presenting a psychological view of morality. For while the moral makeup of individuals depends to a large extent on their determining moral values, which are maintained by the mind and put into practice, their moral behavior becomes largely a response to habitual feelings rather than a deeply intellectual process.

The other ingredient of Wordsworth's psychological statements is truth to experience. He was unblinkingly honest about psychological phenomena, especially those events that happened to himself and even if they weren't flattering. For example, in Book X (1805) of *The Prelude*, the narrator admits that during the Reign of Terror:

> Amid the awe
> Of unintelligible chastisement
> I felt a kind of sympathy with power. . . .
>
> (414–16)

In view of all the "enormities" of the massacres that Wordsworth laments, the admission of sympathy with the perpetrators comes as a shock, even though it is accompanied by admiration for his honesty.

Because of his honesty and moral penchant, many of his psychological insights have the flavor and force of maxims. The best-known, and for that matter probably the best, is contained in "My Heart Leaps Up":

The Child is father of the Man. . . .

This insight is a larger version of what Freud later said with regard to the establishment of man's sexual nature in early childhood. And of course Wordsworth is right: if physically we are what we eat, psychologically we are what we have thought and felt from birth. Several other examples of succinct insights are that "belief [is] the soul of fact" (*PW*, III, 213) and that "truth is hated, where not loved" (*The Prelude* [1850], VII, 532). Even in his conversation, Wordsworth apparently dealt in epigram: he once told his brother, Christopher, "The mind often does not think, when it thinks that it is thinking."[15]

Among such terse psychological insights, there is a high incidence of paradox, for if one goes very far in plumbing the human mind he will find that many shopworn statements about human behavior are wrong to the point of being the exact contrary of the truth. And immediately we are involved in a new paradox of our own. For paradoxes are by their nature intellectually gritty and seem more at home with writers who are generally considered more cerebral, such as Alexander Pope; it is odd, perhaps, to think of William Wordsworth, with all his emotional appeal, as an aggressive thinker, and yet it is true, although it is not often celebrated.

Probably for this reason Cleanth Brooks, in *The*

Well-Wrought Urn, begins with Wordsworth as an example of his claim that paradox is essential to poetic language; Brooks in fact begins: "His poetry would not appear to promise many examples of the language of paradox."[16] But I believe Brooks is wrong in a number of ways, especially in not seeing that Wordsworth is an *especially* paradoxical poet. There are also his claims that Wordsworth's paradoxical writing is somehow unintentional and that he is merely presenting us with an unfamiliar view of familiar things.[17] On the contrary, Wordsworth's paradoxes deal with the essence of things and show us that we are mistaken in our views.

Even the oxymorons that are part of his style are more than clever turns of phrase, but rather strike at some underlying truth of human life. As we will see in the last chapter, the relationship of pleasure and pain is complex, and so we have expressions such as the "discontent of pleasure" and "sad delight." A great variety of oxymorons are in fact scattered through the poetry: "pleasing fear," "tumultuous harmony," "modest pride," "strenuous idleness"—each makes us stop and consider the truth of the seeming contraries. And again we are reminded of Wordsworth's calling one of his correspondents "a *thinking* writer" and how true it was of himself.[18]

Besides the many statements containing psychological observations and the many, often paradoxical, maxims that can be found in his works, there are whole poems and passages in poems that are devoted to psychological themes or insights. And, again, there are many paradoxes involved.

"Simon Lee" has been variously interpreted; lately a good deal of emphasis has been placed on the manipulation of the response of the reader, and most often the

paradox presented at the end is treated as an afterthought:

> I've heard of hearts unkind, kind deeds
> With coldness still returning;
> Alas! the gratitude of men
> Hath oftener left me mourning.

John Danby, who has, in my opinion, provided the best
close reading of the poem, gives this ending a bit more
prominence: "'Simon Lee' exists as a poem, I think, to
carry these lines to the reader in the precise way it does:
with the weight, the depth, the soberness, the measured
seriousness and overflowing tenderness that they
have."[19] Otherwise, however, Danby sees the poem as
an attempt to change the reader's attitude toward Simon
and toward life in general, with the end simply func-
tioning within that design.

I would like to argue, on the contrary, that, considering Wordsworth's penchant for finding paradoxes in
human nature, the point of the poem is actually the ending itself. Not that our attitude toward Simon Lee is unimportant or has not been progressively worked upon,
but despite all the space devoted to his description
Simon really exists in the poem to point up the pathos
of the paradox, for without sufficient build-up, the paradox would at best seem forced, at worst unintelligible.
Wordsworth himself seems almost embarrassed at the
sixty lines of introduction and takes twelve more (ll. 61–
72) to apologize for the lack of a narrative to follow.

John Danby himself doesn't seem to have understood
the paradox:

> What, for example, we might be moved to press
> on the poet, what is there in "gratitude" to lead

to "mourning"? But what in a case like this can the poet tell us that we don't know already, and that his poem has not already put us in the way to realize? The answer might include reference to the iniquities of society and the harshness of Time in its dealings with men. Both these references the poem makes. What mourning is it, though, that supervenes on the young man's vigorous health and good spirits, and goes even deeper than the tears that are brought to the eyes of a helpless old man? The question is best left rhetorical. [20]

The mourning of the narrator may indeed include all these large-scale feelings, although I'm not sure where the poem makes "references" to them. But the paradox, which is fascinating in its overturning our preconceptions about gratitude and ingratitude, can be explained without them. Paradoxes by nature are always explicable, but often to explain one is like explaining a poem (and here I believe we are doing both): the explanation very much lacks the force of the original itself. In any case, ingratitude can make us mourn (for what "man has made of man"), but the effusive and disproportionate *gratitude* of someone who is unable to help himself may make us mourn even more about the human condition. Such an insight is surely enough to support an entire short poem.

A further example of a moderately lengthy (sixty-line) short poem, "Anecdote for Fathers," is likewise built around a simple, but quite interesting, psychological observation, which, although not paradoxical, nevertheless also required considerable introduction. A small boy is brow-beaten by a narrator to explain a personal preference based on an intuition. Perhaps because of its title, "Anecdote for Fathers" is most often interpreted as telling us an interesting fact about child psychology.[21] But the poem has a wider meaning than that; in fact it has two observations to convey. One is that the intuitions of adults or children cannot be explained, at least in a normal, rational fashion, and the other is that if forced to explain the inexplicable, most people will finally lie to escape the pressure. If the poem's meaning is at all determined by age, an additional point might be that children are easier to bully.

A final example of a poem given over totally to psychological probing is the little-known "Star-Gazers." The poem begins with a description of a "Show-man" and his telescope and a crowd lined up to look through it, and it ends with a description of the viewers as appearing "less happy than before" and seemingly "dissatisfied"—even though before viewing they were impatient and envious of the customer at the telescope. Such an unexpected result piques the narrator's curiosity; and the rest of the poem, the middle five stanzas, looks at possible explanations, ten of them. After quickly dismissing the first five, physical possibilities,[22] such as the use of an inferior instrument or bad eyesight, he gets into the psychological explanations, each more interesting than the last. He asks at first: ". . . Gives a thing but small delight that never can be dear?," *or*, do we only like what is expensive? And next:

> Or is it rather that Conceit rapacious is and strong,
> And bounty never yields so much but it seems to
>   do her wrong?

In other words, is the reward of viewing the vastness of space less than the offense to our vanity (conceit)? And then—possibility number eight—perhaps the soul after a "journey long" must be sad on its return. Or maybe "men of the multitude" simply aren't up to the experience (number nine); the narrator rejects this elitist explanation vigorously, with a general statement: "men thirst for power and majesty!"

Finally, and most persuasively:

> Does, then, a deep and earnest thought
>   the blissful mind employ
> Of him who gazes, or has gazed? a grave
>   and steady joy,
> That doth reject all show of pride, admits
>   no outward sign,
> Because not of this noisy world, but silent
>   and divine!

This tenth alternative involves an oxymoron, "a grave and steady joy"—not joy as we usually think of it, exultant and lively. Such a serious joy, the narrator tells us, could be expected because it is "silent and divine" as a result of the uplifting experience, and thus the joyful people only *appear* unhappy and dissatisfied. Perhaps the reason this interesting poem has received so little acclaim is its poor organization, with the explanations offered before the problem is presented; the bouncy, facile versification likewise cannot have helped to attract readers.

Besides such psychological poems, there are also passages that present incidents or observations in passing. In Book VI of *The Prelude*, in a passage that first reminisces on a visit to the Lake District on summer holiday from Cambridge and that lists the various persons who were present—his sister and Mary Hutchinson—Wordsworth then records the kind of illusion in retrospect that happens to all of us (ll. 246–48):

> O friend, we had not seen thee at that time,
> And yet a power is on me and a strong
> Confusion, and I seem to plant thee there.

Coleridge *should* have been there, and so the memory places him there.

In a sonnet on the impending war with France, "October, 1803" ("These Times"), we are told without explanation that "rich men [are] brave by nature" but "that riches are akin / To fear, to change, to cowardice, and death." On its face, the latter statement is easy to accept, but seems to make the former statement harder to understand, for the first explanation of it that comes to mind is that the rich must be brave to defend their amassed possessions, and the second statement denies that. An alternative explanation to the paradox might be that rich men must be brave and aggressive to become rich in the first place, but that the threat of losing it all unmans them nonetheless.

Two late poems comment on the effect of environment on the human psyche. In "At Furness Abbey" ("Well have"), railway workers choose the grounds of the abbey to eat their lunch:

> They sit, they walk
> Among the Ruins, but no idle talk
> Is heard; to grave demeanor all are bound. . . .

The phenomena is often encountered when visiting religious ruins: "All seem to feel the spirit of the place." The other instance (in "To the Moon") of effect of the

environment on the mind is more difficult to understand, at least the paradox at the end of the passage addressed to the moon (ll. 31–39):

> And lives there one, . . .
> One, who has watched thee at some quiet hour
> Enthroned aloft in undisputed power . . .
> [And not] sometimes felt a fitness in thy sway
> To call up thoughts that shun the glare of day,
> And make the serious happier than the gay?

The moon in the given situation makes profound
thoughts easier to entertain and thus makes the thinker
happier than his thoughtless neighbor—two insights in
the guise of one.

Some of Wordsworth's interest in the mind concerned simple sense perceptions. As we saw in Chapter
I, Wordsworth told Aubrey de Vere that the swan in the
lines, "The swan on still St. Mary's Lake / Floats double,
swan and shadow" ("Yarrow Unvisited") could not have
been plural because of the visual effect.[23] Another similar image in "Written in March" has no comment recorded about it:

> . . . The cattle are grazing,
> Their heads never raising;
> There are forty feeding like one!

In such a light-hearted poem, this image is perhaps easy
to overlook, but the truth of the observation will come
home should you come across a similar scene with cows
in one unobstructed view and distant enough to be seen
together. The cows, probably because they are all doing
the same thing (Wordsworth seems to be explaining as

well as describing), appear in an odd way to be one animal. Seeing, however, is believing.

A sonnet with a similar phenomenon is "With Ships the sea was sprinkled far and nigh," and fortunately Wordsworth offered an explanation as he did of the swans. In the poem the narrator picks out one ship from a variety in the scene before him:

> This Ship was naught to me, nor I to her,
> Yet I pursued her with a Lover's look;
> This Ship to all the rest did I prefer. . . .

Wordsworth explained to Lady Beaumont in defense of the sonnet:

> . . . who is there that has not felt that the mind can have no rest among a multitude of objects, of which it either cannot make one whole, or from which it cannot single out one individual, whereupon may be concentrated the attention divided among or distracted by a multitude? After a certain time we must either select one image or object, which must put out of view the rest wholly, or must subordinate them to itself while it stands forth as a Head. . . .[24]

Here the psychological phenomenon is at the center of the poem, but Wordsworth offers no explanation to the general reader, who must therefore judge the psychological truth of the description as it stands.

One last example of the mind's dealings with perceptions concerns the general instance of the effect of ruins on the mind compared with incompleted structures. In "Malham Cove," Wordsworth confronts a nat-

ural semicircle of three tiers shaped like an amphithea-
tre, which, he laments, is not a complete circle,
concluding:

          . . . 'mid the wreck of IS and WAS,
Things incomplete and purposes betrayed
Make sadder transits o'er thought's optic glass
Than noblest objects utterly decayed.

Sometimes the poet simply leaves the reader pondering
the truth of his clearly presented observations, as I believe is the case here.

There is another group of poems that deal with the
mind's facility for associating objects or events. Wordsworth, as we saw in Chapter II, does not exhibit in his
works (or letters and reported conversations for that
matter) much interest in associationist psychology beyond explaining some elemental workings of the mind.
But he did notice how the mind sometimes put things
together on an individual basis, and like so many other
things psychological these instances interested him sufficiently to turn them into poems.

"Strange Fits of Passion," is perhaps the best example of one of these poems of association. Unlike the
other Lucy Poems, this poem has been correctly interpreted a number of times, and there seems little dis-
agreement today on the main point of the poem. The
speaker, who is in love with Lucy, is riding toward her
cottage when an optical illusion causes the moon to appear to set behind it as he and his horse approach. He is
riding along in a reverie with his eye on the moon when
it "sets" suddenly, and he relates the moon's setting to
Lucy's possible death:

What fond and wayward thoughts will slide
Into a Lover's head!
"O mercy!" to myself I cried,
"If Lucy should be dead!"

It is indeed a "fond and wayward" thought, but the immediate "cause" is not difficult to grasp, and the dreamlike state makes the incident easy to believe as well.

A similar poem, with a star instead of the moon, is the sonnet "It is no Spirit," which is less interesting probably in being less subtle. The evening star is apostrophized as "O most ambitious Star!" and the association of the first star to appear at night with ambition is complete when the speaker comments:

And, while I gazed, there came to me a thought
That I might step beyond my natural race
As thou seem'st now to do. . . .

More interesting is another sonnet, "Where lies the Land," which, like the sonnet on the ship discussed above, features the narrator discussing a single ship under way and wondering aloud at its destination. In the sestet he repeats the question:

Yet still I ask, what haven is her mark?
And, almost as it was when ships were rare,
(From time to time, like Pilgrims, here and there
Crossing the waters) doubt, and something dark,
Of the old Sea some reverential fear,
Is with me at thy farewell, joyous Bark!

The murky thought pattern from indeterminent destination to the era of maritime discovery to the doubt and fear attendant on those times is what makes this a more interesting poem.

Sonnets seem to have lent themselves to conveying such psychological incidents; the last example at least is another sonnet, "To the Torrent at the Devil's Bridge, North Wales, 1824." Here we have an address to a stream that is running with such force that the speaker imagines that it cannot "issue from a British source":

> There I seem to stand,
> As in life's morn; permitted to behold,
> From the dread chasm, woods climbing
>   above woods,
> In pomp that fades not; everlasting snows;
> And skies that ne'er relinquish their repose;
> Such power possess the family of floods
> Over the minds of Poets, young or old!

In fact, the association seems to have taken the old poet back to the Gorge of Gondo, which as a young poet he descended after having crossed the Simplon pass (*Prelude*, [1805], VI, 556–61):

> The immeasurable height
> Of woods decaying, never to be decayed,
> The stationary blasts of waterfalls,
> And everywhere along the hollow rent
> Winds thwarting winds, bewildered and forlorn,
> The torrents shooting from the clear blue sky. . . .

Here the association is simply with the past ("life's morn"), but what a remarkable past!

While interest in the psychology of ordinary, normal people was active throughout his life, Wordsworth seems to have been interested in abnormal psychology early and to have lost interest fairly soon. In fact with one or two exceptions all the poems that deal with abnormal mental states were written by mid-1798; indeed, even by the completion of *The Borderers* in February, 1797, the interest had all but disappeared. "The Thorn" was the only important poem after that to deal with mental aberration.

There was in any event an early interest in such abnormal states of mind; there are pertinent passages in *An Evening Walk* and "Salisbury Plain" and the shorter psychodramas, such as "The Mad Mother" and "The Complaint of the Forsaken Indian Woman." That these are not well-known, or are unknown altogether except to specialists, provides a good indication that Wordsworth had little talent for dealing with the abnormal, although his contemporaries seemed to admire his efforts along these lines.[25] Perhaps Wordsworth's and their common heritage in the eighteenth-century sentimental tradition explains their admiration. Be that as it may, few writers have succeeded to any degree with abnormal psychology this side of madness; Shakespeare and Dostoyevsky come immediately to mind, but the list isn't long.

James Averill, who set forth the details of the sentimental tradition, also notes Wordsworth's use of Erasmus Darwin's treatment of various forms of mental disorder in his *Zoonomia* (1794–96).[26] Wordsworth's familiarity with Darwin's work is proven beyond doubt by his use of *Zoonomia* for the actual "facts" of "Goody Blake and Harry Gill"; indeed, in a note to the poem Wordsworth cites Darwin and emphasizes what he considers the factual nature of the story.

In Volume II of *Zoonomia; or, The Laws of Organic*

Life, Part II—"Containing a Catalogue of Diseases Distributed into Natural Classes According to Their Approximate Causes with Their Subsequent Orders, Genera and Species, and with Their Methods of Cure"—the story of "Goody Blake and Harry Gill" appears under Class III, "Diseases of Volition," Species 1, "*Mania Mutabilis*. Mutable Madness," a problem of hallucination; it is the seventh and last case given and appears pretty much the way it does in the poem. I have set forth this information in detail in order to confront a claim made by Averill that Wordsworth follows "Darwin's case history approach."[27] Donald Davie had made a similar claim years before, but without consideration of Darwin: ". . . Many of [Wordsworth's] poems are the records of his experiments, cases to go into his casebook."[28]

Both these scholars, however, seem to me to be missing the great difference between Wordsworth's psychology and that of doctors like Darwin. As a physician writing a medical treatise, Darwin was only interested in the abnormal, in the sick mind; and the categorizing of aberrations, to which the case-history method belongs, was a standard approach in medical texts, used by Darwin's cited sources, William Cullen and Francois Sauvages.[29] Darwin presents the various cases as illustrations of the different species of madness, while Wordsworth, on the other hand, gives stories of isolated incidents that help us to understand the mind better. He does not offer the stories as illustrative case studies but for their own intrinsic interest. On the face of it, this may seem a small distinction; it does in fact constitute a major difference and helps us to see more clearly what Wordsworth is trying to do.

Averill discovers the possible source of several other

of Wordsworth's psychological observations in Darwin's *Zoonomia*: a detail in "The Mad Mother" and a remark about parenting that he applies to "The Last of the Flock."[30] An observation by Darwin about the uses of math and science for relieving mental distress seems also to have found its way into *The Prelude*, and Averill claims that aspects of sentimental love that have turned to madness provide the psychological underpinnings of "The Mad Mother," "Ruth," and "The Thorn."[31] There are other possible points of Darwinian influence on Wordsworth not remarked by Averill that will be mentioned in the following discussion.

But what Averill misses of greater importance is how much Wordsworth relies on Darwin for comments and details of incidents and characters involved in *abnormal* psychology, whereas Wordsworth relies almost totally on his own observation and theorizing for what he says about normal, healthy states of mind. This point perhaps indicates where Wordsworth's real bent and talents lie, despite Averill's claims to the contrary.

The madness of sentimental love, or "erotomania" as Darwin also calls it, might well fit the case of Vaudracour in Wordsworth's poem, "Vaudracour and Julia." There is, however, nothing particularly appropriate to the poem in Darwin's description, but then Vaudracour does not fit the usual pattern given by Darwin; his is not a case of unrequited love but rather one of parental interference; and yet the result is the same. On the other hand, Vaudracour does seek solitude, as Darwin would have predicted, and reaches what Darwin calls the "irremediable" stage, becoming finally "an imbecile mind" (line 306).[32]

Darwin saw erotomania as operative in both life and art, and most of his examples are taken from literature, appropriate in an age that still saw literature as an imitation of life. James Averill disagrees:

> The disappointed lover described here [in Darwin] is rather more a literary than a psychological type. In real life people usually compromise their desires, where in literature, the extremes of sentiment sweep away an Ophelia or an Othello. Indeed, Darwin's primary examples of this pathology are from literary texts. He cites Romeo and Juliet, Virgil's Dido, and Ovid's Medea as sufferers from the "disease."[33]

Averill is clearly contrasting life and art—here "literary" versus "psychological"—and it is clear as well that in his opinion Shakespeare was not a realistic writer, at least in the examples cited. And, of course, Darwin, whom Averill sees generally as scientific in method, is also being challenged in the passage quoted.

Wordsworth, however, just as clearly threw his lot in with Darwin and Shakespeare, for he insists in the short preface to "Vaudracour and Julia" on the factual basis of his story, as does his note dictated to Isabella Fenwick. And in the poem itself he makes the literary connection, obviously linking the psychological or realistic with the literary as compatible, even mutually supportive (ll. 87–91):

> I pass the raptures of the pair;—such theme
> Is, by innumerable poets, touched
> In more delightful verse than skill of mine
> Could fashion; chiefly by that darling bard
> Who told of Juliet and her Romeo. . . .

Whether or not Wordsworth's story is also a sublimation of his own affair with Annette Vallon is beside the point, except perhaps in deepening the truth of the portrayal of Vaudracour's attachment.

The one example of erotomania that Darwin takes from life was the madness of Martha Ray, a famous actress, whose name Wordsworth gave to the heroine of "The Thorn." Such a connection gives James Averill all the more reason to bring up erotomania with regard to that heroine, but there is another of Darwin's diseases of volition operating in the poem, as we shall see in a moment.

"The Thorn" has had a very uneven career both in critical reputation and interpretation. The central interpretive question has resolved itself into whether the poem is about the narrator or about Martha Ray's story or both.

My own understanding of the poem is closest to the interpretations of Stephen M. Parrish and W.J.B. Owen, who see the poem's central concern as the psychology of the mariner narrating the poem.[34] I would join with them in arguing that there is no good reason for ignoring the stated intention of the poet as given in a note to the poem in 1800:

> . . . It appeared to me proper to select a character
> . . . to exhibit some of the general laws by which
> superstitition acts upon the mind. Superstitious
> men are almost always men of slow faculties and
> deep feelings; their minds are not loose, but ad-
> hesive; they have a reasonable share of imagina-
> tion. . . . It was my wish in this poem to show
> the manner in which such men cleave to the same
> ideas; and to follow the turns of passion, always

different, yet not palpably different, by which
their conversation is swayed. I had two objects to
attain; first, to represent a picture which should
not be unimpressive, yet consistent with the
character that should describe it; secondly, while
I adhered to the style in which such persons describe, to take care that words, which in their
minds are impregnated with passion, should
likewise convey passion to Readers who are not
accustomed to sympathize with men feeling in
that manner or using such language.

The "picture which should not be unimpressive" quite
clearly takes second place to "the character who should
describe it." In fact, as Parrish argues, the poem is a
dramatic monologue.

But "dramatic monologue" is misleading if taken to
mean that the only interest in the poem is the psychology of the narrator, for there are different kinds of dramatic monologue. "The Thorn" is more like Brown-
ing's "My Last Duchess" than his "The Bishop Orders
His Tomb"; that is, there is an equal interest in the story
told in the monologue. In fact, the comparison is illuminating: the stories told in "The Thorn" and in "My
Last Duchess" are interesting to the extent that uncer-
tainties arouse the curiosity of the reader about what has
happened.

There is, however, a note dictated to Isabella Fenwick about the poem that has been used to point up the
prime importance of the thorn bush itself and the story
of the person it so clearly represents:

Alfoxden. 1798. Arose out of my observing, on
the ridge of Quantock Hill, on a stormy day, a

thorn which I had often passed in calm and bright weather without noticing it. I said to myself, "Cannot I by some invention do as much to make this Thorn permanently an impressive object as the storm has made it to my eyes at this moment?" I began the poem accordingly, and composed it with great rapidity.

But those who use this note to prove the primacy of the story do not consider that Wordsworth is here describing the genesis of the poem, not its meaning, which is given in the note (quoted above) to the poem.

The genesis is fascinating in itself if we speculate for a moment and put the pieces together. Wordsworth apparently started by composing a thirteen-line verse description of the thorn preserved in the Alfoxden Notebook.[35] Then, as W.J.B.Owen and Mary Jacobus point out, traditional ballads and other poems that Wordsworth knew that involved thorns also contained unwed mothers and infanticide.[36] Reinforcing the choice of story, James Averill argues, is the eighteenth-century equivalence of the "sublime emotions" of seeing the thorn in the storm to the "tragic feelings" of the story of Martha Ray.[37] Averill continues: "Attempting to convey the significance and impressiveness of this one thornbush among millions, it seemed natural for him to give up the labors of description and to invest the thorn with the kind of substitutive excitement available in human suffering." It must have been at this point that Wordsworth, having chosen a suitable story to make the thorn impressive, chose the main point of the poem, as put in The Preface to *Lyrical Ballads*: "to make these incidents and situations interesting by tracing in them, truly though not ostentatiously, the primary laws of our nature"—in this case the workings of the superstitious mind of the narrator.[38]

After describing the background of the narrator in the 1800 note to the poem, Wordsworth remarked that "such men, having little to do, become *credulous* and talkative from indolence . . ." (italics added). Darwin may have had something to offer the poet here as well, for he has another species of mania he calls "credulitas."[39]

Credulity is a mental disorder of "decreased volition" and seems to be an almost universal mental problem rather than a form of outright insanity, for Darwin begins: "Life is short, opportunities of knowledge rare; our senses are fallacious, our reasonings uncertain, mankind therefore struggles with perpetual error from the cradle to the coffin."[40] "Ignorance and credulity have ever been companions," he adds a little later and then lists instances of credulity, including witchcraft, "the fictions of fancy," astrology, and apparitions. Credulous people, he also observes, "as having less knowledge of nature, and less facility of voluntary exertion, would more readily believe the assertions of others, or a single fact, as presented to his own observation."[41] The narrator of "The Thorn" readily believes both.

Darwin lists as one "great source of error" of credulity "the vivacity of our ideas of imagination," and we remember that Wordsworth says of superstitious men that "they have a reasonable share of imagination."[42] Indeed, W.J.B.Owen speculates that perhaps superstition is simply a form of imagination.[43] Owen also finds "credulous" to be part of an encyclopedia definition of superstition, noting that it is also "Wordsworth's word in his note to the poem," and then he goes on to discuss for several pages the kind of half-belief of the narrator's superstition, his "fascinated uncertainty," which Owen suggests is the "kind of superstitious mind which Wordsworth wants to portray."[44] Owen apparently finds the portrait, as I do, much more interesting than the sort of superstitious minds displayed by the villagers.

But, to return to the critical reputation of the poem, is the portrait of the narrator in this dramatic monologue a success? When you have just reconsidered the interpretations of a poem and come to a new understanding of your own, it is all too easy to see that poem as better than it is. The poem does seem to me better now than in the past, and yet I wonder if there is sufficient depth possible in the psychology of superstition itself to hold a reader's interest for 242 lines. It is this question rather than the poet's efforts to convey his vacillation and garrulousness—which seem to me on the whole successful—that is probably at the heart of the poem's at least partial failure.

Wordsworth wrote "The Thorn" in the spring of 1798, just as his interest in abnormal psychology was drawing to a close and as he was in his letters and conversation both openly disapproving of the exploitation of emotions and deliberately trying to avoid it in his writing.[45] Part of the process of such avoidance, documented by James Averill, involved the turning from emphasis on incident to the kind of scrutiny of character we have been examining in this chapter.[46]

But during the same period in which "The Thorn" was composed Wordsworth was still both showing an interest in abnormal psychology and to an extent exploiting emotional interest in the extravagant by presenting, in such poems as "Her Eyes Are Wild" and "The Complaint of the Forsaken Indian Woman," char-

acters who were either mad or suffering from great
emotional distress. Like "The Thorn," both poems have
been said to verge upon dramatic monologues,[47] and
Coleridge in a notebook entry remarked on the psychological realism of a passage in "Her Eyes Are
Wild,"specifically the last two of the following lines:

> About that tight and deadly band
> I feel thy little fingers prest.
> The breeze I see is in the tree;
> It comes to cool my babe and me.

Coleridge praised the last two lines as

> so expressive of that deranged state, in which
> from the increased sensibility the sufferer's atten-
> tion is abruptly drawn off by every trifle, and in
> the same instant plucked back again by the one
> despotic thought, and bringing home with it, by
> the blending, *fusing* power of Imagination and
> Passion, the alien object to which it had been so
> abruptly diverted, no longer an alien but an ally
> and an inmate.[48]

Such was apparently the way Wordsworth meant both
poems to be read, for in the Preface to *Lyrical Ballads* he
claimed the purpose of both poems was "to follow the
fluxes and refluxes of the mind when agitated by the
great and simple affections of our nature."[49]

Whatever the aim of the poem and whether or not
he was again exploiting emotions, the poems seem to
me failures, perhaps because, given in the first person,
the emotions aroused spill over into sentimentality or
because the eccentric madness portrayed does not lend

itself to the universalizing function of art. William Bagehot once remarked that the mad character of Meg Merrilies in Scott's novel, *Guy Mannering*, had been built up
slowly:

> This is the only way in which the fundamental
> objection to making eccentricity the subject of
> artistic treatment can be obviated. Monstrosity
> ceases to be such when we discern the laws of
> nature which evolve it: when a real science ex-
> plains its phenomena, we find that it is in strict
> accordance with what we call the natural type,
> but that some rare adjunct or uncommon casu-
> alty has interfered and distorted a nature, which
> is really the same, into a phenomena which is al-
> together different. Just so with eccentricity in hu-
> man character; it becomes a topic of literary art
> only when its identity with the ordinary princi-
> ples of human nature is exhibited in the midst of,
> and as it were, by means of, the superficial un-
> likeness. Such a skill, however, requires an easy
> careless familiarity with the usual human life and
> common human conduct.[50]

Wordsworth, I've been arguing all along, had the
necessary familiarity with "common human conduct,"
but he had no room in the short poems in question to
paint the portraits slowly. He seems to have realized
eventually that madness, or even near madness, is too
eccentric to be represented briefly in literature, for, by
the time he wrote "Ruth" later in the same year, he had
already dropped the first-person mode and the attempt
to present a dramatic monologue; Ruth becomes "mad,
/ And in a prison housed" but her mind is not portrayed

in any detail. And the last of Wordsworth's mad mothers, who appears in a late poem, "The Widow on Windermere Side" (1837?) is presented as a portrait not to be scrutinized for our edification, but rather to convey a paradox, namely that there is no need to pray for the happiness of the insane in the next life for they are happier than we are *now*.

But before these poems on madness were written, Wordsworth created his most sustained psychological portrait of an abnormal character, that of Oswald in *The Borderers*. Nothing like the subtlety nor complexity of Oswald exists in Darwin's catalogue of mental aberrations, and the critical response has been appropriately large. Considering its reputation as a dramatic failure, the play has attracted a disproportionate amount of scholarship, most of it directed toward Oswald; to date there have been at least seventeen articles, as well as chapters and parts of chapters in other Wordsworthian studies.[51] Wordsworth would no doubt have welcomed such attention, for he himself wrote an analytical essay on Oswald that runs about two thousand words. There is no question at least that Oswald is his most ambitious attempt at the psychological study of a character.

Most scholars have seen Oswald as the center of the play and have examined at length his psychological make-up and motivations in the play and their possible sources in literature and life, especially Shakespeare's Iago, various Gothic literary villains, and Wordsworth himself during the French Revolution and the moral crisis that followed. The range of treatment of Oswald can be gathered simply by a look at the designations used: "a Machiavellian villain," "a revolutionary superman," "clear-eyed intellectualized evil," "an introspective egoist," "an embodiment of anarchic energies," "a bloody-minded revolutionary," and "an existentialist manqué."

Although the scholarship contains constant allusions to Wordworth's stated intentions as conveyed in the introductory essay (1798), the prefatory note to the published play (1842), and the note dictated to Isabella Fenwick (1843), those explicit intentions have never to my knowledge been the focus used to examine Oswald's character.[52] As was the case with Wordsworth's note on "The Thorn," it seems ill-considered to take what one wants from Wordsworth's explanations and to ignore the rest of what he gave of his intentions, although, if one takes Wordsworth whole hog, one should beware the intentional fallacy in the process. The question to bear in mind is whether Wordsworth accomplished what he intended, or at least whether what he said was in the play *was* in the play.

For, although analysis of Oswald's character based mostly on the play itself, as well as the examination of possible sources and even of the degree to which his character was shaped by the requirements of the play, are all useful endeavors, they can also mislead. Wordsworth clearly was creating a character as well as writing a play or reflecting his reading or working out his own problems; and there is sufficient evidence in the essay and notes, I believe, to make a case that the plot was fashioned for Oswald and not Oswald for the plot. Wordsworth, moreover, seems to argue in the essay that Oswald's philosophy and morality were likewise fashioned by his psychology, the real point of the play and the direct result of his thoughts and actions before and after the play starts. In this regard, the question whether Oswald is a Godwinian (the focus of a great deal of attention) is interesting but irrelevant.

The reason behind Wordsworth's unusual attempts
to explain in prose his most complex character is not
difficult to see; his explanations seem to have been stim-
ulated by reaction to the play. *The Borderers* was rejected
by Covent Garden reportedly for the "metaphysical obscurity" of Oswald,[53] and when the revised version was
published in 1842 a reviewer found Oswald "too much
on the extreme of evil."[54] Wordsworth wrote in the same
year that he feared Oswald's portrait would be considered "too depraved for anything but biographical writing."[55] All three quotations demonstrate that a problem
existed; the latter two further suggest that Oswald was
not considered sufficiently generalized, that his characterization may have been possible ("biographical") but
not probable, as Aristotle would have put it. The same
objection was raised by critics about Byron's Conrad in
The Corsair—a tender-hearted lover and cut-throat
pirate[56]—as well as Meg Merrilies, as we saw earlier.
With Oswald of course there was no question of outright madness but rather abnormally evil behavior.

I suspect, in any event, from what we have seen of
Wordsworth's other ready psychological explanations of
his poems, that he could have explained at some length
the make-up of every character in the play, although
there is no question that Oswald was the central character for the playwright. In the essay, Wordsworth said
the delineation of Oswald, and presumably the play as a
whole, was intended "to shew the dangerous use which
may be made of reason when a man has committed a
great crime" (154–56). He explained in his following
two paragraphs that he wished to make the audience
aware of what had become all too familiar, "moral sentiments . . . applied to vicious purposes" (157–59).[57]

Morality is clearly mixed with psychology in both

of these stated endeavors, as in the play itself, and the morality presents its own problems. For the initial evil deeds of both Oswald and his victim, Marmaduke—the parallel murders by exposure that set Oswald to further evil and Marmaduke to extreme remorse—were not, I would argue, really evil deeds at all, inasmuch as in both cases the men were tricked into commission of the deed, which presumably they would not have done otherwise and which both did with the best of motives. Orthodox Christianity, most legal systems, and indeed a simple sense of justice require deliberate acquiesence in what would be a crime in order for guilt to be incurred—accidental killing, for example, is not considered the crime of manslaughter unless irresponsibility is involved.[58] Even the sin of presumption (the crime of kangaroo justice) is ruled out here by the need in the context of the play for the private administration of justice in the absence of law. Only Oswald's fraudulent betrayal of Marmaduke, which Wordsworth specifies that Oswald was "deliberately prosecuting" (Essay, 117–18), constitutes an evil deed, and it is this evil deed that seems to require Wordworth's explanation.

Oswald's own betrayal by his fellow mariners shows him not to have been a fundamentally evil man and consequently more interesting. But there are weaknesses in "the very constitution of his character" (Essay, 147) that turn his "great intellectual powers" (Essay, 1) to evil purposes when the proper catalyst is present. Wordsworth chooses as Oswald's "master passions" pride (the sin of Satan) and "the love of distinction," which here in its evil guise might be simply called vanity (Essay, 2–3). Wordsworth adds to these qualities two more efficient goads to action, a certain "restlessness" (Essay, 21) and an experimental bent that has no limits (Essay, 149–

50). Benevolence, a final check on all these potentially evil traits, is missing (Essay, 2), and we end with a portrait that has a familiar ring to it. At this level of generalization, it might with few modifications fit many white-collar criminals and twentieth-century dictators.

The catalyst was the murder of the captain—not in itself an immoral deed for Oswald—that set his weaknesses in motion. The subsequent evolution of Oswald's corruption is similarly described by Oswald in the play[59] and by Wordsworth in his essay, the two versions differing only in that the latter is more complete. And although the essay itself, like so many of Wordsworth's prose works, does not hang together well, the history of Oswald's psychological corruption is clear enough if implicit connections are attended to.

His betrayal to mutiny and "murder" has the immediate consequence of failure and loss of influence (Essay, 25–26; *Borderers*, 1760–63),[60] which in the absence of benevolence leads to disgust and misanthropy and, upon his withdrawal from the world, to a radical examination of morality. His guilt or need for consolation thereupon leads the examination naturally to cynicism and moral skepticism; when left to our own devices, Wordsworth demonstrates, how easily we turn morality into what we want it to be.

At this point, Wordsworth tells us through Oswald's mouth as well as in the essay that restlessness brings him back into the world, and continuing guilt leads him to both evil actions and renewed moral speculation. This search for "relief from two sources" (Essay, 22) constitutes in fact Oswald's main complexity; his mixture of the strongly pragmatic and widely contemplative is remarked upon by Marmaduke:

That a man

So used to suit his language to the time,
Should thus so widely differ from himself—
It is most strange.

(ll. 1568–71)

C. J. Smith, commenting on the necessity for Oswald not only to be active in "poisoning" Marmaduke's emotions, but also to be "a man capable of *reasoning* his victim into a murder," concluded that Oswald was "an impossible character-creation."[61] Such people as Oswald with his unusual combination, as Byron's Conrad with his, are real but admittedly rare.

At least the self-justification Oswald indulges in is not difficult to grasp. And there is a realistic, modern note in Oswald's resorting to anthropology for rationalizations,[62] as well as in his eventual reliance on subjective morality, a sort of moral relativism that co-exists, as so often in real life, with a constant and conflicting appeal to an absolutist concept of justice.[63] The consequence is moral bankruptcy; morality is finally perverted by reason—the "dangerous use" Wordsworth is so interested in demonstrating.

After Oswald's weaknesses have come to fruition at the beginning of the play but before he commits what Wordsworth calls his "apparently motiveless crime," three motives have in fact been given in the play (and two of these are given in the Essay, 101–104): Marmaduke had saved Oswald's life and "gratitude's a heavy burden/To a proud Soul" (see also lines 918–21); Marmaduke was chosen over Oswald to be leader of the band (lines 551–53); and, if we can believe Oswald himself, he sought "for sympathy" (lines 1864–66) and wished to free Marmaduke from the fetters of conven-

tional morality (lines 1855–58). Despite all these motives and the observation "that such a mind by very
slight external motives may be led to the commission of
the greatest enormities" (Essay, 104–106), Wordsworth,
and apparently his critics, felt that there were insufficient "malignant injuries" (Essay, 120) on Marmaduke's
part to account for Oswald's crime of betrayal.

At this point I should say a word about the extent of
Wordsworth's reliance on Shakespeare's Iago, for the
question is raised by discussion of a motiveless crime.
Wordsworth's use of Iago as a model for Oswald is mentioned so frequently by scholars that it is assumed to be
true, and the usual implications are that Oswald is a
kind of pale copy of Iago, in much the same way that
many of Shelley's characters in *The Cenci* are copies of
Shakespeare originals.[64] But the scholars who look more
closely at the resemblance most often conclude that
while there are similarities between Oswald and Iago
there are still greater differences between them and that
Wordsworth's attempt transcends Shakespeare's character.[65] It is unfortunate that the original view prevails, for
it obstructs any effort to see what Wordsworth actually
attempted and accomplished.

Faced with the problem of a seeming insufficiency
of motivation, in any case, Wordsworth offered subtler
considerations that possess the depth and originality of
paradox. First, deriving from what Wordsworth saw as
Oswald's inevitable "unnatural" appetite for "strange-
ness" (Essay, 86, 92), "the non-existence of a *common*
motive" (italics added) or the "love of the marvelous"
(Essay, 122–23, 125) becomes "itself a motive to action"
(Essay, 123).[66] Secondly, Oswald "hates the more
deeply because he feels he ought not to hate" (Essay,
131). Thirdly, dissatisfaction with itself causes the

mind, not to turn from evil, but to proceed to more guilt, for "uneasiness must be driven away by more uneasiness" (Essay, 134–35). Finally, every new evil deed sets remorse at defiance and seems to widen options (even as it narrows them). And at the end of the Essay, Wordsworth provides two additional considerations: that originally trivial motives are often left behind in the evolution of a serious deed and that we often "apply our own moral sentiments as a measure of the conduct of others" (Essay, 182–83), whereas their own minds have been busy contorting the moral dimensions of their behavior.

The first four of these psychological phenomena are evident in the play itself, although by their nature Oswald cannot be aware of them. Along with the history of the evolution of his corruption, furthermore, they contract the portrait into more of an individual and less of a generic model and support the probability of a single prototype encountered during the French Revolution—twice mentioned by Wordsworth himself as the occasion for his observations.[67] But such a prototype, of course, was not essential and there are sufficient universal aspects to Oswald's make-up for his actions to seem easily believable to us after the Holocaust and its enormities of evil consorting with the otherwise normal behavior of its perpetrators.

As we have seen, Wordsworth had a habit of carefully considering the psychology underlying his works and of explaining it when called upon. There doesn't seem to be any question that Oswald was conceived of as a complex character, and I have argued that he can be understood in Wordsworth's own terms. Oswald was not simply an evil man, certainly not simply a too-evil man, as the 1842 reviewer claimed. Oswald has all the complexity of a human who has been brought to an extremity of evil by the multiple weaknesses of his character and certain subtle psychological forces set in motion by external events. All the gothicism and melodrama of the play ought not to be allowed to obscure that complexity and the limited success of the characterization.

It may be that Wordsworth himself finally considered Oswald a failure and consequently dropped any further serious attempts at abnormal psychology, for we have already noted that by the time *The Borderers* was written such attempts had all but ceased. But there is evidence in the Fenwick note ("I cannot think upon a very late review that I have failed") and in the ultimate printing of the play that more than likely Wordsworth considered the portrayal a success and then went on to the *more* difficult task of dealing with normal psychology and the shepherds, beggars, and leech gatherers that body it forth.

NOTES

1. James Averill, *Wordsworth and the Poetry of Human Suffering* (Ithaca, NY, 1980), p. 148.
2. Averill, pp. 10, 56. An impression of the same view is given by chapters 1–2 of Alan Bewell's *Wordsworth and the Enlightenment* (New Haven, 1989).
3. Donald Davie, ed., *Selected Poems of William Wordsworth* (London, 1962), pp. 25–26. See also W. J. B. Owen, *Wordsworth as Critic* (Toronto, 1969), p. 108.
4. Ernest de Selincourt, ed., *The Letters of William and Dorothy Wordsworth: The Middle Years, Part I*, second edition, revised by Mary Moorman (Oxford, 1969), II, 148. Hereafter cited as *Letters: Middle Years*.
5. A. B. Grosart, ed., *The Prose Works of William Wordsworth* (London, 1896), III, 437.
6. Ernest de Selincourt, ed., *The Letters of William and Dorothy Words-*

worth: *The Early Years*, second edition, revised by Chester L. Shaver (Oxford, 1967), I, 587. Hereafter cited as *Letters: Early Years*.

7. *Letters: Early Years*, I, 234.
8. *Letters: Early Years*, I, 314.
9. See the note dictated by Wordsworth to Isabella Fenwick on "The Childless Father": "When I was a child at Cockermouth, no funeral took place without a basin filled with sprigs of boxwood being placed upon a table covered with a white cloth in front of the house." A bough was taken by each mourner, carried to the burial spot, and then thrown into the grave.
10. David Ferry, *The Limits of Mortality* (Middletown, Conn., 1959), p. 64.
11. Grosart, III, 465.
12. W. J. B. Owen and J. W. Smyser, eds., *The Prose Works of William Wordsworth* (Oxford, 1974), I, 103.
13. Owen and Smyser, I, 126.
14. John Hayden, *Polestar of the Ancients* (Newark, 1979), p. 177.
15. Grosart, III, 460.
16. Cleanth Brooks, *The Well-Wrought Urn* (New York, 1947), p. 3.
17. Brooks, pp. 5–7.
18. Ernest de Selincourt, ed., *The Letters of William and Dorothy Wordsworth: The Later Years*, second edition, rev. by Alan G. Hill (Oxford, 1979), V, 714.
19. John Danby, *The Simple Wordsworth* (New York, 1961), p. 38.
20. Danby, p. 47.
21. See especially Mary Jacobus, *Tradition and Experiment in Wordsworth's* Lyrical Ballads *(1798)* (Oxford, 1976), pp. 101–103.
22. Actually, the order of the explanations is slightly different than given here.
23. Grosart, III, 487–88.
24. *Letters: Middle Years*, II, 148. The explanation continues:

> I am represented in the Sonnet as casting my eyes over the sea, sprinkled with a multitude of Ships, like the heavens with stars, my mind may be supposed to float up and down among them in a kind of dreamy indifference with respect either to this or that one, only in a pleasurable state of feeling with respect to the whole prospect. "Joyously it showed," this continued till that feeling may be supposed to have passed away, and a kind of comparative listlessness or apathy to have succeeded, as at this line, "Some veering up and down, one knew

not why." All at once, while I am in this state, comes
forth an object, an individual, and my mind, sleepy and
unfixed, is awakened and fastened in a moment. . . .
This Ship . . . in its own appearance and attributes . . .
is barely sufficiently distinguish[ed] to rouse the creative
faculty of the human mind; to exertions at all times welcome, but doubly so when they come upon us when in
a state of remissness. The mind being once fixed and
rouzed, all the rest comes from itself; it is merely a
lordly Ship, nothing more:

> This ship was nought to me, nor I to her,
> Yet I pursued her with a lover's look.

My mind wantons with grateful joy in the exercise of its
own powers, and, loving its own creation,

> This ship to all the rest I did prefer,

making her a sovereign or a regent, and thus giving
body and life to all the rest; mingling up this idea with
fondness and praise—

> Where she comes the winds must stir;

and concluding the whole with

> On went She, and due north her journey took.

Thus taking up again the Reader with whom I began,
letting him know how long I must have watched this
favorite Vessel, and inviting him to rest his mind as mine
is resting.

25. Samuel Taylor Coleridge, *Biographia Literaria*, chap. XXII; *PW*, I,
330; A. R. Waller and Arnold Glover, eds., *The Collected Works of
William Hazlitt* (London, 1902–1904), XII, 270. Alan Bewell is a
modern admirer: he called (p. 157) "The Mad Mother" "one of the
most powerful . . . poems of *Lyrical Ballads*. . . ."
26. Averill, pp. 153–59, 166–68.
27. Averill, p. 156.
28. Davie, p. 25. See also Alan Bewell, p. 91.
29. Dr. William Cullen, *Synopsis Nosologiae Methodica* (1818); Francois
Sauvages, *Nosologia Methodica* (1768).
30. Averill, pp. 156–57. This application, however, seems to me mistaken.

31. Averill, pp. 157–58, 167.
32. Erasmus Darwin, *Zoonomia* (London, 1794–96), II, 365.
33. Averill, p. 167.
34. Stephen M. Parrish, " 'The Thorn': Wordsworth's Dramatic Monologue," *ELH*, 24 (1957), 153–63; W. J. B. Owen, " 'The Thorn' and the Poet's Intention" *The Wordsworth Circle*, 8 (1977), 3–17.
35. Quoted in Jacobus, p. 241.
36. Jacobus, pp. 241–242; Owen, p. 8.
37. Averill, p. 179.
38. Owen and Smyser, I, 123.
39. Darwin, II, 408–11.
40. Darwin, II, 408.
41. Darwin, II, 410.
42. Darwin, II, 409.
43. Owen, p. 15,
44. Owen, pp. 10, 13, 11.
45. Averill, chapter 6.
46. Averill, pp. 207–13.
47. Parrish, p. 155.
48. Coleridge, *Biographia Literaria*, chap. XXII.
49. Owen and Smyser, I, 126.
50. Walter Bagehot, *The Collected Works of Water Bagehot*, ed. Norman St. John-Stevas (Cambridge, Mass, 1965), II, 56.
51. For a list of the articles and chapters through 1969, see Robert Osborn, "Meaningful Obscurity: The Antecedents and Character of Rivers," in *Bicentenary Wordsworth Studies*, ed. Jonathan Wordsworth (Ithaca, N.Y.and London, 1970), notes to pp. 394–95.
52. The three items appear in Robert Osborn, ed., *The Borderers* (Ithaca, N.Y.and London, 1982). All citations to the items will refer to this edition and to the line numbers as given there.
53. *Letters: Early Years*, I, 197n.
54. *The Athenaeum*, 27 August 1842, p. 758.
55. *Letters: Later Years* VII, 320.
56. John O. Hayden, *The Romantic Reviewers* (Chicago, 1969), pp. 139–40.
57. Something like this attempt to illuminate the familiar is claimed for Wordsworth's part in *Lyrical Ballads* by S. T. Coleridge in the second paragraph of Chapter XII, *Biographia Literaria*: Wordsworth was to awaken the reader "from the lethargy of custom."
58. So-called "sentimental morality," based solely on feeling, might explain the feelings of guilt, for, when trickery is discovered, one

is likely to *feel* guilty (even if one is not responsible) because of the innocence of the victim and the "remorse" at one's own gullibility. But such an explanation cannot hold for the playwright.

59. Especially in Act IV, scene ii (Osborn's divisions).

60. The points, as I have claimed, occur in both the essay and the play, but it would be tedious to continue citations.

61. Charles J. Smith, "The Effect of Shakespeare's Influence on Wordsworth's 'The Borderers,' " *SP* 50 (1953), 632. Robert Osborn ("Meaningful Obscurity," p. 399) claims Oswald's polarities are hypocrisy and sincerity, which terms fit his actions and meditations respectively.

62. Essay, pp. 69–73: ". . . Whenever upon looking back upon past ages, or in surveying the practices of different countries in the age in which he lives, he finds such contrarieties as seem to affect the principles of *morals*, he exults over his discovery and applies it to his heart as the dearest of his consolations."

63. Oswald uses the word "justice" seven times in the play, most often in an appeal to its authority and several times repeating it within a few lines. The most obvious instance of inconsistent yoking of absolutist and relativist beliefs occurs in ll. 595–598:

> Happy we are,
> Who live in these disputed tracts, that own
> No law but what each man makes for himself;
> Here justice has indeed a field of triumph.

64. F. R. Leavis, *Revaluation* (New York, 1963), pp. 223–227.

65. Smith, pp. 631–32; Roger Sharrock, "*The Borderers*: Wordsworth on the Moral Frontier," *Durham University Journal*, 25 (1964), 175–76; Osborn, "Meaningful Obscurity," pp. 399–400; Ernest de Selincourt, *Oxford Lectures on Poetry* (Oxford, 1934), p. 175.

66. This first motive given by Wordsworth (Essay, pp. 122–28) may be interpreted as the absence itself of a motive. Such is the suggestion afforded by Wallace, a member of the band: "Natures such as his/ Spin motives out of their bowels. . . ." (lines 1427–28) and seems to be the interpretation given by W. J. B. Owen and J. W. Smyser, eds., *The Prose Works of William Wordsworth* (Oxford, 1974), I, 84. But such would be a strange claim by Wordsworth in view of the number of motives given in the play and in the Essay itself.

67. In the Preface of 1842 and the Fenwick note.

IV

Wordsworth And The Psychology Of Literature, Creativity, And Imagination

William Wordsworth had the sort of curious mind that ranged widely over a good number of interests, moral, social, political. It is not surprising, then, that as a poet he turned to literary theory and to the creativity involved in literature. And by now it should also be no surprise if his interests were largely psychological in basis.

Contrary to the received view of William Wordsworth as a Romantic expressionist, he was in reality a traditional Aristotelian in his basic literary theories. The main document in this regard is the famous Preface to *Lyrical Ballads*, contained in every anthology of literary criticism, but in fact his theory doesn't change in later works in any significant way.

Wordsworth believed in a set of critical principles, for as he wrote in 1802, "Without an appeal to laws and principles there can be no criticism."[1] These principles he shared with most of his contemporaries, including both Samuel Taylor Coleridge and the reviewers of his own volumes,[2] but since I have dealt with this matter elsewhere, I will not render a full treatment here.[3]

And yet this membership in a tradition is worth reinforcing and is in any event essential here as a basis for discussing Wordsworth's original contributions both to the principles of that tradition and to related issues. As for traditional mimesis, the truthful representation of human experience, Wordsworth says bluntly, "Poetry is the image of man and nature," and in the same paragraph adds the complementary principle of universality, making clear his allegiance by direct ascription: "Aristotle, I have been told, has said, that Poetry is the most philosophic of all writing: it is so: its object is truth, not individual and local, but general, and operative . . ." (I, 139).

In the same vein, Wordsworth goes on to claim—sounding like an echo of Dr. Johnson—that the poet "converses with general nature" (I, 140). On this point he contrasts the scientist, who converses only "with those particular parts of nature which are the objects of his studies." This universalizing side of literature, the unifying side, is stressed by further contrast of poet and scientist in a passage of the Preface that follows (I, 141; italics added):

> Poetry is the breath and finer spirit of *all* knowledge; it is the impassioned expression which is the countenance of *all* Science. Emphatically may it be said of the Poet, as Shakspeare hath said of man, "that he looks before and after." He is the rock of defence for human nature; an upholder and preserver, carrying everywhere with him re-

lationship and love. In spite of difference of soil
and climate, of language and manners, of laws
and customs: in spite of things silently gone out
of mind, and things violently destroyed; the Poet
binds together by passion and knowledge the
vast empire of human society, as it is spread over
the whole earth, and over all time.

Unlike the scientist, who divides and analyzes, the poet
performs the universalizing function described in Chapter IX of the *Poetics*.

Following directly out of this traditional universal
aspect of literature, Wordsworth's next comments almost seem directed toward those who wish to see him
as a pioneer expressionist, except that of course by 1802
that concept had hardly been verbalized, much less re-
futed, by anyone. The poet, he claimed, does not differ
"in kind from other men, but only in degree," and the
thoughts and feelings he has "are the general passions
and thoughts and feelings of men." The poet does not
express "his feelings for his own gratification, or that of
men like himself." No, "Poets do not write for Poets
alone, but for men" (I, 142–43). Wordsworth's poet can
hardly be mistaken for a lamp casting its beams for its
own purposes, although his creative theory, which we
will deal with later, has misled some scholars to think
so.[4]

No critical tradition, however, can stay vital by simply handing down principles; these must receive new applications and need to be scrutinized and refined.
Wordsworth made one of the largest contributions of
any critic in the tradition before or since, and the psychological bent seen elsewhere in his thought is prominent here as well.

The moral purpose of literature, which can only be found by implication in the *Poetics*, was added to the traditional principles by Horace as part of his formula that the poet both teaches and pleases. As the principle of moral teaching was passed down, it became a rather crude matter of the poet conveying moral truths by precept and example, especially the latter, as can be seen in Sidney and Dr.Johnson.[5] Wordsworth, however, all but eschews the Horatian formula and instead considers the actual moral psychology involved.

First of all, he considers the matter as regards the poet. The "worthy *purpose*" he claims for the *Lyrical Ballads* was not the result of any deliberate self-conscious effort on the part of the poet, but rather resulted from "habits of meditation" the poet can encourage (I, 125, 127). The pertinent passage is associationist and depends on a view of the connection of feeling with thought that is shared with Hume and Kant (and John Dennis) but, according to Mary Warnock,[6] probably derives directly from Wordsworth's own experience (I, 127):

> For our continued influxes of feeling are modified and directed by our thoughts, which are indeed the representatives of all our past feelings; and, as by contemplating the relation of these general representatives to each other, we discover what is really important to men, so, by the repetition and continuance of this act, our feelings will be connected with important subjects, till at length, if we be originally possessed of much sensibility, such habits of mind will be produced, that, by obeying blindly and mechanically the impulses of those habits, we shall describe objects, and utter sentiments, of such a nature, and

in such connection with each other, that the understanding of the Reader must necessarily be in some degree enlightened, and his affections strengthened and purified.

By such a continual process of the scrutiny of his own thoughts and feelings the poet can become habituated to thinking and feeling morally and hence can "teach" the reader. The importance of the passage lies in the moral effect on the reader at the end: ". . . The understanding of the Reader must necessarily be in some degree enlightened, and his affections strengthened and purified." Clearly the process of the moral thinking and feeling of the poet is conveyed through the poem to the moral thinking and feeling of the reader and this conveyance "must necessarily" be the case, if only, he qualifies quickly, "in some degree."

We have obviously moved away from the rather crude notion of a reader considering, for example, Aeneas carrying Anchises from burning Troy and thinking to himself, "I would like to be like that." Now we have an unconscious and inevitable moral effect on the reader; he will be enlightened and will understand human experience better and have healthier feelings and thus become a better moral agent. This concept of moral indirection also appears in his letters to John Wilson (1802) and to Charles James Fox (1801), as well as later (1816) in his *Letter to a Friend of Robert Burns* (". . . Though there was no moral purpose [in a Burns' poem], there is a moral effect" [III, 124]).[7]

Pleasure, the other side of the Horatian formula, also receives psychological treatment at Wordsworth's hands. Already of considerable prominence in Dr. Johnson's criticism, in the Preface pleasure becomes "a particular purpose" of the poet, and we are told that "The Poet writes under one restriction only, namely, the necessity of giving immediate pleasure to a human being . . ." (I, 138–39).[8] As is also the case with Dr.Johnson, Wordsworth's hedonism must be placed in the context of his moral views or it will seem out of its real proportion.

In any event, Wordsworth defends his strong hedonism as no "degradation of the poet's art" but as a necessary result, for literature reflects in an "indirect" way both "the beauty of the universe" and "the native and naked dignity of man" and thus *must* please the reader (I, 140). Then Wordsworth appeals to "the grand elementary principle of pleasure," which explains all human life, especially man's sympathy and knowledge. Wordsworth may simply be following Aristotle's pronouncement that happiness is the aim of all human actions, for pleasure seems equated with happiness as a universal motive, just as it is equated by John Dennis in his *The Usefulness of the Stage*.[9]

If so, Wordsworth may be doing no more than psychologically linking pleasure with his moral teaching through motive, perhaps even breaking down the distinctions between goodness and happiness within some basic psychological theory of happiness. There is enough evidence of some such theory to become the subject of a small book by H. C. Duffin, who saw Wordsworth as offering a theory prefiguring the "systematic study of happiness" of such modern writers as "Dr. Lin Yu Tang and Mr. J. C. Powys, Bertrand Russell and Hermann Keyserling."[10] Happiness in this context also seems related to the concept of Joy, treated in my final chapter.

In his psychological re-examination of traditional

literary principles, in any event, Wordsworth turned to
the issue of feeling as a link between human experience
and the poet and between the poet and the reader.
Wordsworth, as we have seen, seems to have almost
taken for granted the basic validity of mimesis and universality. But the poet, whom the tradition had all but
ignored, Wordsworth found to be the key to the subordinate issues of subject and style, especially through the
vehicle of the poet's feelings.

We have also seen the poet treated as a kind of
"trained feeler" when Wordsworth dealt with the morality of literature. He further considered the poet "as in
the situation of a translator" (I, 139) between nature,
including natural passions, and the reader. Such emphases on feelings suggest the new Romantic stress on feeling evident by the late eighteenth century, and documented by Walter J. Bate[11]; and of course Wordsworth
was influenced by his times; but the immediate reasons
are, I believe, more psychological and subtle.

From another slant, Wordsworth's new emphases on
feeling can also be seen as reactionary, as part of his psychological reassessment of literary principles. For from
the time of Aristotle, with his categorizing bent, theorists in the tradition had dealt with literature on the more
practical level largely through the categories of genres
and the complementary principle of decorum (that the
style fit the genre). Originally the determination of style
by genre was presumably natural, as Wordsworth himself implies in the *Preface of 1815* (III, 27), but later the
relationship became codified, and subjects consequently
became more limited. Certain subjects, as well as certain
styles, that is, eventually became "poetical."

It is significant, therefore, that Wordsworth doesn't
so much as mention genres in the Preface to *Lyrical Bal-*

lads. When he does offer the customary list of genres later in the *Preface of 1815*, moreover, he changes immediately to a psychological view, "to the powers of mind *predominant* in the production of them" (III, 28) and to subject matter as the method of categorization of his poems in the 1815 edition. It may have been a time ripe for such ignoring of genres, for Robert Mayo, who examined the magazine verse of the 1790s, concluded that "great confusion with respect to traditional literary genres" then obtained.[12]

Whatever the situation, Wordsworth in the Preface to *Lyrical Ballads* replaced genre and decorum with a new principle based on feeling that harkens back to what must have been the original psychology of poetic creation: that "the feeling . . . developed gives importance to the action and situation, and not the action and situation to the feeling" (I, 129).[13] No longer, Wordsworth was saying in effect, was it necessary to have a coronation or a heroic action for the subject of a serious poem. You could choose "incidents and situations from common life" (I, 123); subjects concerning idiot boys and little girls would be excellent choices as long as the poet infused them with the necessary feeling. In fact, in his choice of subjects for *Lyrical Ballads*, Wordsworth was not just choosing low subjects, but almost totally insignificant ones, such as incidents involving beggars and mad mothers. He was, one could say, pushing his principle as far as it would go.

If Robert Mayo finds similar subject matter in a "persistent minority" of magazine verse of the 1790s it is not surprising.[14] The ballads of both the magazine verse and of *Lyrical Ballads* are a natural outgrowth of the ballad revival of the late eighteenth century, but Wordsworth was not just proposing his poems as innocuous ballad imitations but rather as legitimate poems in their own right. He was not lowering the worth of his efforts, but raising the status of the ballad. As a matter of fact, what was revolutionary, as Coleridge later pointed out,[15] was not Wordsworth's practice but his argument that any subject matter could be used in poems in the mainstream of English poetry, not just in ballad imitations — at least he doesn't qualify his comments in that direction.

The ballad form (along with the poems of Robert Burns) showed the possibility of some other way of writing poetry beyond the "hackneyed elegies, odes, occasional poems" that Mayo mostly found in the magazines of the time.[16] Even though traditional ballads were considered a crude and unsophisticated genre (if even a "genre"), they treated elemental though "more humble subjects" (I, 145); they were consequently an obvious choice as a vehicle for experimenting with subject matter. Ballads, moreover, are listed in the *Preface of 1815* as a type of lyric (III, 27), and lyric was another genre that offered a field for experimentation, since it also had never fit the genre scheme well, from Aristotle through the Renaissance theorists.

And so, starting with the title *Lyrical Ballads*, Wordsworth was out to subvert the whole idea of genres. In the edition of 1800, he also described several poems in their titles as "a pastoral," another as "a conversation," and another as "a description." The first, pastoral, was a traditional genre but the poems he offers under that rubric hardly fit into it, and the others were not traditional genres at all. John Jordan, in his study of *Lyrical Ballads* (1798) remarks, moreover, that Wordsworth was "exceedingly and uncommonly chary of any genre designations . . . ," especially compared to contempo-

rary volumes, which "seem typically genre con-
scious."[17]

The issue of choice of subject matter is not commonly considered the revolutionary aspect of the Preface to *Lyrical Ballads*; most scholars seem to have agreed
with W. J. B. Owen that its "main object . . . is to define
and defend a particular rhetoric. . . ."[18] Yet I believe style
can be seen as secondary to subject and not only because
style was dependent on subject in Wordsworth's scheme.
He goes on immediately after the "formula" given above
to mention the importance of the issue he has raised,
speaking gravely about the mind's capability to be ex-
cited "without the application of gross and violent stim-
ulants" (I, 129) and he then discusses the high importance of enlarging the capability, especially in the face of
the contemporary influences he thought were diminish-
ing it.

By comparison, in fact, the question of style seems
almost an afterthought despite the space allotted to it.
When Wordsworth looked back in 1815 to the Preface
to *Lyrical Ballads*, he mentions first "the feelings which
had determined the choice of the subjects" and *secondly*
"the principles which had regulated the composition of
those Pieces . . ." (III, 26n). The reviewers of the volume, it is worth adding, attacked the subject matter
more often than the style.

Poetic style, especially diction, was of course also a
part of the topic of the Preface, and Wordsworth's style
was also attacked by reviewers. Indeed, style and subject
matter are especially closely connected in Wordsworth's
scheme, as we have seen. Style, moreover, has its own
importance, for if a "poetical" style is all that is available
to the writer of a serious poem, then it won't matter
much what the subject is. Such a style will subvert any

but a "poetically acceptable" subject by a simple inept-
ness. The poetical style itself, therefore, had to be confronted and eliminated.

First of all, Wordsworth simply rejects poeticisms,
what he calls the "family language" (I, 131) of poets—
part of the conventional high style that evolved to fit into
the old scheme of decorum of genre. Such language is
found widely in eighteenth-century poetry and, although Wordsworth only specifies excessive personifi-
cation (I, 131), it also includes the compound epithets
Coleridge attempted to rid from his early poetry,[19] the
neologisms formed by making nouns into adjectives by
adding "y" (lawny, sheety), and the circumlocutions so
popular at the time.

These mannerisms of the age are at their worst in the
many third-rate imitators, but they can even be found in
abundance in such important poems as Thomson's *The
Seasons*, Goldsmith's *Deserted Village*, and Collins' "Ode
to Evening." Such a "mechanical device of style" (I,
131) paradoxically began as "arbitrary and capricious
habits of expressions" (I, 125) but became "mechanical"
or conventional over time. Again Wordsworth is reactionary in wanting to go back beyond the eighteenth
century to Milton and Shakespeare (I, 129). If only he
had said clearly what it was he was rejecting, instead of
trying to offer positive phrasings of what he wanted
("the very language of men," "the language of prose
when prose is well written" [I, 131, 133]), he might have
made a better case and have avoided a good deal of controversy.

For Wordsworth not only rejected the poetical style,
but he offered as an alternative a positive process that is
both reactionary in aim and psychological in design and
again takes the shape of a sort of "formula" (I, 137):

. . . If the Poet's subject be judiciously chosen, it will naturally, and upon fit occasion, lead him to passions the language of which, if selected truly and judiciously, must necessarily be dignified and variegated, and alive with metaphors and figures.

That is, the choice of subject will determine the feeling that will determine the style.

This is, of course, the very psychological process at the basis of decorum, but over the years the process had been short-circuited so that in the eighteenth century the formula could have been restated: the subject/ genre will determine the style. And because of the consequent importance of a high subject for the required high style of any poetry that was to be taken seriously, the choice of subjects had become severely limited.

By going back to psychological roots, Wordsworth was able to take even a potentially embarrassing subject such as the love of a mother for her idiot son and transform it through his feeling into a successful, light-hearted poem. As he later reported of "The Idiot Boy" to Isabella Fenwick, he "never wrote anything with so much glee." Even a more serious theme, such as a young girl's rejection of death as a divisive factor, need only be treated seriously, not solemnly; the badgering narrator of "We are Seven" is almost comic in his obtuseness. And in "Dejection: An Ode" Coleridge offers as evidence of the necessity of joy for creativity the instance of Wordsworth's converting the potentially painful story of Lucy Gray into a successful poem once it was "tempered with delight" (line 119).[20]

The emphasis on the poet and his feelings as the center of the process, however, brought its own problems, for feelings are less manageable than a mere literary convention such as decorum had become. We have already seen that Wordsworth was concerned with the emotional corruption of the times, but perhaps a longer passage would not be out of place here (I, 129):

> For a multitude of causes, unknown to former times, are now acting with a combined force to blunt the discriminating powers of the mind, and, unfitting it for all voluntary exertion, to reduce it to a state of almost savage torpor. The most effective of these causes are the great national events which are daily taking place, and the increasing accumulation of men in cities, where the uniformity of their occupations produces a craving for extraordinary incident, which the rapid communication of intelligence hourly gratifies. To this tendency of life and manners the literature and theatrical exhibitions of the country have conformed themselves.

He goes on to speak of "the magnitude of the general evil," which he claimed he was doing his best to combat.

The poet himself, of course, is also at risk. He is vulnerable at both points on the formula, subject to feeling and feeling to style (I, 153):

> I am sensible that my associations must have sometimes been particular instead of general, and that, consequently, giving to things a false importance, I may have sometimes written upon unworthy subjects; but I am less apprehensive on

this account, than that my language may frequently have suffered from those arbitrary connections of feelings and ideas with particular words and phrases, from which no man can altogether protect himself.

Subjects, that is, may have been connected with abnormal feelings in the poet; or his feelings may have been connected with abnormal connotations of language. And he adds gravely a few lines later: the poet's "own feelings are his stay and support. . . ."

In the general emotional corruption of the times, the reader was even less likely to be unscathed than the poet. A number of qualifications Wordsworth makes show that he believed the healthy emotions of readers could not be taken for granted; at one point he qualifies, "if [the reader] be in a healthful state of association" (1800, I, 126) and at another, "if his Reader's mind be sound and vigorous" (I, 151). This was a serious consideration, for if the reader's feelings were unsound, poetry could neither have its moral effect nor give much pleasure. A lot depended on the reader as the apt receiver of the translation from nature and natural passions offered by the poet. Wordsworth also wished to consider "how far [the present state of the public taste in this country] is healthy or depraved" (I, 121), for if a good number of readers were affected by corrupted feelings, a serious breakdown would occur.

Whether or not Wordsworth was an alarmist on this matter of emotional corruption could easily be the subject of an entire monograph, but it is worth considering briefly here. Wordsworth himself mentions the brutalizing effects of new phenomena, such as urbanization and large scale wars (I, 129). By the end of the eighteenth century, it could be argued, the "dissociation of sensibility" described by T.S. Eliot was well under way, and the "frantic novels, sickly and stupid German Tragedies, and deluges of idle and extravagant stories in verse" (I, 129) that Wordsworth offers as evidence existed in abundance, as well as, presumably, the "degrading thirst after outrageous stimulation" (I, 129–131) that they were pandering to. One can only wonder what Wordsworth would have said had he seen what was coming.

In view of his concern, in any event, it is not surprising that he scrutinized the psychology of creation, which so involves the feelings. There is actually very little theory about the very act of composition but what there is is well known (I, 127):

> For all good poetry is the spontaneous overflow of powerful feelings: and though this be true, Poems to which any value can be attached were never produced on any variety of subjects but by a man who, being possessed of more than usual organic sensibility, had also thought long and deeply.

A complementary passage occurring later in the Preface reads (I, 149):

> I have said that poetry is the spontaneous overflow of powerful feelings: it takes its origin from emotion recollected in tranquility: the emotion is contemplated till, by a species of re-action, the tranquility gradually disappears, and an emotion, kindred to that which was before the subject of contemplation, is gradually produced, and does

itself actually exist in the mind. In this mood successful composition generally begins, and in a
mood similar to this it is carried on; but the emotion, of whatever kind, and in whatever degree,
from various causes, is qualified by various pleasures, so that in describing any passions whatsoever, which are voluntarily described, the mind
will, upon the whole, be in a state of enjoyment.

It is clear that this theory of composition concerns the
second part of the formula, the movement from feeling
to style; the subject has already been chosen, and we are
dealing with what Croce would call the expression.

The necessary ingredients for this creative act are,
first of all, the specific emotions elicited by the subject;
these are central and immediate. Then, Wordsworth
points out in the first quotation, there must be thought
and sensibility as the necessary equipment of the poet,
his by good fortune and by cultivation. These ingredients undergo a process outlined in the second quotation:
there must be a passage of time; and the eventual recollection must not be forced, but rather must be sponta-
neous; and it must take place in tranquility and will be
accompanied by pleasure.

The emotions that overflow are of course the feelings
central to the formula, and the requirement of thought
may have been Wordsworth's way of eliminating the idea
of Romantic emoting, although there is really no reason
to suppose thinking was not part of the process as he
experienced it, especially since he was such an intellectual poet. It is balanced, in any case, by the qualification
of spontaneity, which eliminates the contrary idea that
one can write deliberately at any time he wishes.

Likewise, while there are possible sources for the requirement of recollection,[21] it also may have simply been part of his experience, and in any case it is difficult to think of a successful poem being composed while in the grip of a strong emotion. The tranquility and pleasure—calm and joy—that are part of the process, moreover, seem to make the creation of poetry similar to the visionary experience, for as we will see in the last chapter, calm and joy are also essential for Vision. Coleridge's remarks about the need for the story of "Lucy Gray" to be "tempered with delight" (quoted above) indicate that he agreed about the necessity for calm and joy in the process of creation.

The result of placing all the above ingredients in the process is that emotions "kindred" to the original gradually appear and composition begins. These emotions involved in the creation of a poem "are indeed far from being the same as those produced by real events," we are told later (I, 138), and yet are closer to those real-life emotions than "other men are accustomed to feel in themselves," presumably in real-life situations. This "disposition to be affected more than other men by absent things as if they were present" is also part of the poet's equipment and may be one function of the imagination, although it is not called by that name here.

According to James Heffernan, who has studied Wordsworth's "transforming imagination," Wordsworth moved from feeling to imagination as "the chief source of poetry," although feeling remained as "the motive power, energizing the imagination. . . ."[22] It is true that imagination is only briefly mentioned three times in the Preface to *Lyrical Ballads* (1802), yet by 1802 the concept of imagination was present in the Preface where the term itself is not used.[23] In any event, imagination in its literary functions became a central concern of the *Preface of 1815.*

In the eighteenth century, imagination and fancy had been used indiscriminately to refer to the same faculty,[24] but by 1815 much controversy had occurred and Wordsworth felt it necessary to offer contrasting definitions of the two at considerable length. Like Coleridge, Wordsworth rejected the etymology of the words and then extended the meaning "far beyond the point to which philosophy would have confined them" because of "poverty of language," as he explains in the *Essay Supplementary* (III, 81).

Set adrift from etymology and aiming toward newly extended meanings, neither Wordsworth nor Coleridge are cautious, as one might expect, but rather become quite assertive. Both, in fact, act as if the imagination were something one could point to, like a water buffalo. Without etymologies or general usage, one can offer his own definition of a term but can hardly quarrel with someone else's—as Wordsworth does with William Taylor's and with Coleridge's and as Coleridge does with his. There must have been at least some larger contemporary usage both have in mind, but neither refers to any.[25] It begins to have all the flavor of an intellectual game with no rules.

There is, however, a possible explanation for the efforts at redefinition. It could be that for Wordsworth, and for Coleridge, it's neither the term nor the faculty (qua faculty) that they're concerned with, but rather the concept of poetic creativity behind them, especially inasmuch as the eighteenth century was more or less limited to seeing poetic creativity in the terms Wordsworth and Coleridge apply to fancy. Their new concept of another, higher faculty—the imagination—was perhaps necessary, at least as part of theory, to raise poetic creativity to a new plane and thus give poetry a new importance (again).

Wordsworth, in any case, redefines Imagination for six pages (III, 30–35) as an active faculty that works on poetic material by conferring, abstracting, and modifying—functions he demonstrates by analyzing a number of examples of figures of speech. Imagination works with "the plastic, the pliant, and the indefinite" and changes their constitution, their "inherent and internal, properties" (III, 36). Fancy he then defines as a lesser faculty that brings poetic material together temporarily without changing it. Yet sometimes, he tells us, imagination nonetheless works "with the materials of fancy" (III, 37). Despite all the confident assertiveness, Wordsworth is not entirely clear in his distinctions, but Heffernan probably sums the matter up adequately: imagination involves the "fusion of substances" and fancy the "linking of accidents."[26] And, most importantly perhaps, imagination does something the fancy cannot; it unifies poems.

But imagination is not merely the faculty of artistic creativity for Wordsworth. It had three major functions: it operated in perception, in literary creation (as we have seen), and in visionary experiences. Mary Warnock, a scholar who does not abandon etymology and treats imagination as a philosophical concept linked closely to Hume and Kant, deals with the first two functions as seen by Wordsworth and Coleridge, but only hints at the third, the visionary.

Warnock interprets Coleridge's primary imagination as the faculty involved in everyday perception (p.91). Coleridge believed that the real world existed but that the imagination nevertheless "creates" our perceptions.

Wordsworth essentially agreed with this paradoxical view but not that the mind was totally active; external nature also affected our perceptions.

Warnock offers possible sources for their views. Coleridge, we are told, most likely got the creative role of imagination in perception and the function of the secondary imagination in literary creativity from Schelling (pp. 91–92). Her description of Hume and Kant as moving beyond simple perception, on the other hand, sounds very much like Wordsworth's position: "But our actual experience of the world is neither wholly creative nor wholly a matter of passively receiving what we are given. It is a mixture of both elements" (p. 33). The unifying function of imagination in perception, which can also be found in Schelling, was held by both Coleridge and Wordsworth, by the latter partly on his own (pp. 96, 100, 113).

In similar fashion, Coleridge and Wordsworth shared a belief, also possibly arrived at by each on his own, that the imagination was linked to the feelings and linked the feelings to the understanding, in a way that is not in fact much different from the views of Hume and Kant as well (pp. 102–103). The processes involved are quite complex in Wordsworth's expansion of them; Warnock quotes an early passage from "The Pedlar" (MS E, 1803–1804):

> While yet a child, and long before his time
> He had perceiv'd the presence and the power
> Of greatness, and deep feelings had impress'd
> Great objects on his mind with portraiture
> And colour so distinct that on his mind
> They lay like substances and almost seem'd
> To haunt the bodily sense. He had receiv'd

[(Vigorous in mind by nature as he was)]
A precious gift; for as he grew in years
With these impressions would he still compare
All his ideal stores, his shapes and forms;
And, being still unsatisfied with aught
Of dimmer character, he thence attain'd
An *active* power to fasten images
Upon his brain; and on their pictur'd lines
Intensely brooded, even till they acquir'd
The liveliness of dreams.[27]

Feelings produce "shapes and forms" in the mind from sense perceptions of shapes and forms existing in nature, and both those images existing in the mind and those in nature generate feelings. Warnock continues, "The emotion-laden 'seeing' of the image (whether inner or outer) is identical with 'seeing' the truth, not now only about the image itself, but about it as a representative thing. We learn the nature of things in general from the particular, significant case. And we can see that the case *is* significant, if we can see it as a form, something which can be produced and reproduced by our imagination" (p.116). She goes on to support this extension by quoting from the first fifty lines of "Tintern Abbey."

The borderland between the role of the imagination in perception and its role in the visionary experience is a murky area. James Scoggins is correct, in any event, that the ultimate concern of the imagination is transcendental.[28] The unity that the imagination provides to sense perception shades off into the unity of all things.

We will deal with the psychology of Vision in the last chapter, but the twilight area provides room for investigation on its own, for Wordsworth seems to have developed a psychology of unity somewhere between perception and the visionary. And, like so much in Wordsworth's psychology, it is based on paradox.

To begin with, Wordsworth was against divisiveness:

> Enquire of ancient Wisdom; go, demand
> Of mighty Nature, if 'twas ever meant
> That we should pry far off yet be unraised;
> That we should pore, and dwindle as we pore,
> Viewing all objects unremittingly
> In disconnexion dead and spiritless;
> And still dividing, and dividing still,
> Break down all grandeur, still unsatisfied
> With the perverse attempt, while littleness
> May yet become more little, waging thus
> An impious warfare with the very life
> Of our own souls!
>
> > (*The Excursion*, IV, 957–68)

But James Heffernan points out that if Wordsworth had a need for wholeness, he also had a conflicting need for differences; in support he quotes a passage from *The Prelude*: the need to recognize "manifold distinctions, difference / Perceived in things where to the common eye / No difference is . . ." (1805; II, 318–20).

Heffernan is especially insightful in his handling of this area between perception and the visionary: "Clearly, the capacity to distinguish was for Wordsworth an indispensable part of the capacity to relate. Only by immersing itself in endless variety, he believed, could the mind perceive the oneness of nature" (pp. 160–61). Heffernan quotes a very pertinent variant of a line in *The Prelude* ("With difference that makes the likeness clear")[29] before setting forth the central paradox: ". . . The sense of unity arises from a keen perception of diversity," which he immediately rephrases: "*To unite presupposes the ability to distinguish.* Without unity there can be no comprehension, but without multiplicity there is nothing to unite" (p.161). The poet paradoxically "distinguishes in order to relate," and, furthermore, Wordsworth "would not countenance the reduction of the many to the one; he sought to construct the one from the many" (162).

Without such an explanation, the Bartholomew Fair passage of Book VII of *The Prelude* would make little sense. Wordsworth tells us the Fair "lays ...the whole creative powers of man asleep" (679–81) because of its "anarchy and din" (686) and its being "monstrous in colour, motion, shape, sight, sound" (688). After describing at some length the chaos of the booths and sideshows "all jumbled up together" (717), he suddenly stops and offers an explanation:

> Oh, blank confusion! true epitome
> Of what the mighty City is herself
> To thousands upon thousands of her sons,
> Living amid the same perpetual whirl
> Of trivial objects, melted and reduced
> To one identity, by differences
> That have no law, no meaning, and no end—
> Oppression, under which even highest minds
> Must labor, whence the strongest are not free.
> But though the picture weary out the eye,
> By nature an unmanageable sight,
> It is not wholly so to him who looks
> In steadiness, who hath among least things
> An under-sense of greatest; sees the parts
> As parts, but with a feeling of the whole.

Clearly we are beyond simple perception; each of the "trivial objects" is distinctly perceived and yet they are only reduced to one identity without meaning—beyond being "Bartholomew Fair." It is the whole experience that must be given "order and relation" (761) and "ennobling Harmony" (771). Nature provides the necessary education, he tells us, and the faculty so educated, although he does not name it here, is the imagination.

That the imagination provides this first level of unity on the way to the visionary Unity of All Things was an idea Wordsworth shared with Coleridge, but again its genesis is unclear. Heffernan, in any event, quotes one example from Coleridge's letters:

> . . . The universe itself—what but an immense heap of *little* things?—I can contemplate nothing but parts, & parts are all *little*—!—My mind feels as if it ached to behold & know something *great*—something *one* & *indivisible*—and it is only in the faith of this that rocks or waterfalls, mountains or caverns give me the sense of sublimity or majesty!—But in this faith *all things* counterfeit infinity . . . !30

But the notebooks are also a rich source, overlooked by Heffernan, where Coleridge bemoans a failure of imagination. In December, 1804, he wrote:

> O said I as I looked on the blue, yellow, green, & purple green Sea, with all its hollows & swells, & cut-glass surfaces—O what an Ocean of lovely forms!—and I was vexed, teazed, that the sentence sounded like a play of Words. But it was not, the mind within me was struggling to

express the marvellous distinctness & uncon-
founded personality of each of the million millions of forms, & yet the undivided Unity in
which they subsisted.[31]

Down a few lines in the notebook, he mentions the
"aweful adorable omneity in unity" (allness in one).

In the final chapter, we will look at the psychology
of Vision, especially the processes leading up to Vision,
but the last element in that process, insight, should be
examined here at least briefly, since it clearly involves
the faculty of imagination. The most practical and con-
venient way to do so is to examine the Snowdon episode
in the last Book of *The Prelude*, which attempts to describe the visionary dimension of the imagination.

I believe David Ellis is correct that the Snowdon episode was not itself a visionary experience, a "spot of
time," although it is customary to treat it as such.[32] It
seems rather simply the vehicle of an analogy. The scene
itself is not even an especially rare phenomenon despite
its grandeur; a mountain vista looking down on a sea-
like mist, with noises coming from below it, had been
described by at least three others in the late eighteenth
century and by Wordsworth himself twice in other
poems.[33] Such background knowledge is essential if one
is not to miss the factual basis of what may seem strange
and is certainly dealt with in an unusual fashion:

<blockquote>
I looked about, and lo,
The moon stood naked in the heavens at height
Immense above my head, and on the shore
I found myself of a huge sea of mist,
Which meek and silent rested at my feet.
A hundred hills their dusky backs upheaved
</blockquote>

All over this still ocean, and beyond,
Far, far beyond, the vapours shot themselves
In headlands, tongues, and promontory shapes,
Into the sea, the real sea, that seemed
To dwindle and give up its majesty,
Usurped upon as far as sight could reach.
Meanwhile, the moon looked down upon this shew
In single glory, and we stood, the mist
Touching our very feet; and from the shore
At distance not the third part of a mile
Was a blue chasm, a fracture in the vapour,
A deep and gloomy breathing-place, through which
Mounted the roar of waters, torrents, streams
Innumerable, roaring with one voice.
The universal spectacle throughout
Was shaped for admiration and delight,
Grand in itself alone, but in that breach
Through which the homeless voice of waters rose,
That dark deep thoroughfare, had Nature lodged
The soul, the imagination of the whole.

([1805], XIII, 40–65)

This scene contains an extraordinary image of the power of nature to work upon natural objects "for admiration and delight" of human spectators (61).

While the working of this image has been analyzed a number of times, it retains its quite considerable power.[34] The sea of mist becomes a land mass with its own "headlands, tongues, and promontory shapes"; as land, it also has an enormous "chasm" through which sounds come. Then the mist becomes a sea again when the real land below (the hills poking through the mist) becomes a sea-beast (hinted at earlier by "dusky backs upheaved" [45]) with a "breathing-place" and a "roar-ing."

The scene with its protean metaphors seems very like Wordsworth's example (in the *Preface of 1815*) of "images in a conjunction," taken from "Resolution and Independence" (III, 33). There we have an image of a "huge stone" becoming "a sea-beast" and finally an "old man." Analyzing the passage, Wordsworth tells us that "in these images, the conferring, the abstracting, and the modifying powers of the Imagination" are ac-tive. Appropriately, we find out in the next passage of *The Prelude*, where an analogy is set up between the power of Nature and the power of the imagination, that Nature works "upon the outward face of things" and — here Wordsworth uses almost the same words as above — "moulds them, and endues, abstracts, combines" (79). Even the literary imagination works like Nature at times.

It is not necessary, in any case, to take the Snowdon scene as an allegory nor especially to make exact equa-tions between objects on the literal and figurative levels. It is in all probability a real scene with real details, and when the poet has recognized the obvious similarity of the mist to a sea (a comparison made in descriptions by other witnesses) and then notices the odd interlocking movement of apparent sea and land and real sea, as well as the underlying sea-serpent elicited by real roaring sounds and the sight of "backs," he also recognized the power of Nature to make natural objects awesome.[35] He apparently, moreover, calls the chasm in the mist "the soul, the imagination of the whole" (65), because this is the "one object" (81) that Nature (like the imagination in other circumstances) makes "so impress itself / Upon all others, and pervades them so, / That even the grossest minds must see and hear, / And cannot chuse but feel" (81–84).

Then, after a break in the text, Wordsworth draws back and gives us a natural comparison between the scene, which Nature has "shaped for admiration and delight" (61), and a "mighty mind" (70) that also re-shapes Nature for a higher purpose. It is even possible that the grey mist resembles an enormous brain, the physical counterpart of the mind, to help the analogy along. In particular, the scene reminds him of "one function" (74) of the mind, the imagination, that "glorious faculty / Which higher minds bear with them as their own" (89–90).

This is not the secondary, literary function of the imagination; this is not the faculty that combined the interlocking images in the original description of the Snowdon scene, although the two functions are clearly related. We are now come into the area where the visionary imagination makes it possible to intuit the Unity of All, the goal of all visionaries, and thus "to hold communion with the invisible world" (105).

NOTES

1. W. J. B. Owen and Jane W. Smyser, eds., *The Prose Works of William Wordsworth* (Oxford, 1974), I, 164n. Hereafter cited in parentheses in the text.
2. John O. Hayden, "Coleridge, the Reviewers, and Wordsworth," *Studies in Philology*, 68 (1971), 105–19.
3. John O. Hayden, "Wordsworth and Coleridge: Shattered Mirrors, Shining Lamps?," *The Wordsworth Circle*, 12 (1981), 71–81.
4. See especially M. H. Abrams, *The Mirror and the Lamp* (New York, 1953).
5. John O. Hayden, *Polestar of the Ancients* (Cranbury, NJ, 1979), pp. 112–13, 151–53.

6. Mary Warnock, *Imagination* (Berkeley, 1976), pp.102–03; for John Dennis, see Owen and Smyser, *Prose*, I, 170.

7. For the letter to John Wilson, see John Hayden, "William Wordsworth's Letter to John Wilson (1802): A Corrected Version," *The Wordsworth Circle*, XVIII (1987), 37: "But a great Poet ought to do more than this[;] he ought to a certain degree to rectify men's feelings, to give them new compositions of feeling, to render their feelings more sane[,] pure and permanent. . . ." A pertinent passage in the letter to Fox [E. de Selincourt, ed., *The Letters of William and Dorothy Wordsworth: The Early Years*, second ed., rev.by Chester Shaver (Oxford, 1967) I, 315:]: "The poems [in *Lyrical Ballads*] are faithful copies from nature; and I hope, whatever effect they may have upon you, you will at least be able to perceive that they may excite profitable sympathies in many kind and good hearts, and may in some small degree enlarge our feelings of reverence for our species, and our knowledge of human nature. . . ."

8. Hayden, *Polestar*, pp.155–56. See also Dugald Stewart, *Elements of the Philosophy of the Human Mind* (London, 1818), I, 496.

9. E. N. Hooker, ed., *The Critical Works of John Dennis* (Baltimore, 1939), I, 148. "'Tis universally acknowledg'd by Mankind, that happiness consists in Pleasure, which is evident from this, that whatever a Man does, whether in Spiritual or Temporal Affairs, whether in matters of Profit or Diversion, Pleasure is, at least, the chief and the final Motive to it, if it is not the immediate one."

10. *The Way of Happiness* (London, 1947), p. 2. This study is overly effusive, but the quotations brought forward tend to support the following contention about Wordsworth's poetry: "It is not often happy poetry at all; but it is always the poetry of a happy man. It does not contain a philosophy of happiness, or an ethic based on happiness, though it contains materials for both" (p. 1).

11. *From Classic to Romantic* (New York, 1946). See especially Chapter V, "The Growth of Individualism: The Premise of Feeling."

12. Robert Mayo, "The Contemporaneity of the *Lyrical Ballads*," *PMLA*, 69 (1954), 506.

13. There has been some confusion about what Wordsworth meant by his pronouncement and perhaps it would be worthwhile to clarify it. In the 1800 Preface Wordsworth mentions "Poor Susan" and "The Childless Father" as examples of his intent, but the editors of the standard edition (*Prose*, I, 171) apparently interpret Wordsworth to mean that the feelings within the poems ("the emotions which the song of a thrush excites" in the first poem and the "loss

and loneliness" of the father in the second) operate *within* the poem
rather than that the feelings conveyed make the poems important
for the reader. The gist of the following paragraph, however,
makes the meaning clear: ". . . the human mind is capable of excitement without the application of gross and violent stimu-
lants. . . ."

14. Mayo, p. 489
15. James Engell and W. J. Bate, eds., *Biographia Literaria* (Princeton,
    NJ and London, 1983), I, 70–71; II, 8–9.
16. Mayo, p. 489.
17. *Why the* Lyrical Ballads? (Berkeley, 1976), p. 144.
18. W. J. B. Owen, *Wordsworth as Critic* (Toronto, 1969), p. 3.
19. *Biographia Literaria*, I, 6–7.
20. See John O. Hayden, "Coleridge's 'Dejection: An Ode,' " *English
    Studies*, 52 (1971), 1–5.
21. Owen, pp. 52n–53n. See also Stewart, I, 139.
22. James Heffernan, *Wordsworth's Theory of Poetry: The Transforming
    Imagination* (Ithaca, NY, 1969), pp. 109, 58.
23. Warnock, p. 112–113.
24. James Scoggins, *Imagination and Fancy* (Lincoln, Neb., 1966), pp.
    193–194.
25. Some similar contemporary usage can be found in Stewart, I, 287,
    313, 481, 487–88.
26. Heffernan, p. 185.
27. James Butler, ed., *The Ruined Cottage* and *The Pedlar* (Ithaca, NY,
    1979), pp. 392–394 (lines 130–146, "active" italicized by Words-
    worth only in the MS B version [pp. 152–53]). Quoted in War-
    nock, pp. 114–115 with one line omitted (placed here in brackets).
    The Pedlar was first composed in 1798.
28. Scoggins, p. 159.
29. Ernest de Selincourt, ed., *The Prelude*, 2nd ed., rev. Helen Darbi-
    shire (Oxford, 1959), p. 576.
30. Earl L. Griggs, ed., *Collected Letters of Samuel Taylor Coleridge* (Ox-
    ford, 1956), I, 349.
31. Kathleen Coburn, ed., *The Notebooks of Samuel Taylor Coleridge*
    (New York, 1961), II, nr 2344.
32. *Wordsworth, Freud, and the Spots of Time* (Cambridge, England,
    1985), pp. 148–50.
33. James Beattie, *The Minstrel* (1771–74), I, xxi; Ramond, *Lettres de
    M. William Coxe a M. W. Melmoth* (1781)—journey from Engelberg
    to Meiningen; James Clarke, *Survey of the Lakes*, 2nd ed. (1789),

pp. 72–73; *Descriptive Sketches* (1793), II. 494–511; *The Excursion* (1814), II, 829–74. See also Thomas De Quincey, *Literary Reminiscences* (Boston, 1854), p. 314n, where De Quincey reports Wordsworth's claim that he had "repeatedly witnessed" such a scene as that on Mount Snowdon.

34. The most full-blown exposition of the problems supposedly presented by the Snowdon episode, as far as I know, is W. J. B. Owen, "The Perfect Image of a Mighty Mind," *The Wordsworth Circle*, 10 (1979), 3–16. Part of Owen's exposition, however, depends on confusing the visionary function of the imagination here illustrated with the literary function set forth in the *Preface of 1815*—an easy enough confusion to fall into since Wordsworth is using the literary imagination to compare with Nature's similar power to illustrate the visionary imagination. There is also too much attempt made by Owen to work out the "allegory" in detail.

35. One is reminded of the note to "The Thorn," quoted in Chapter III: "I said to myself, 'Cannot I by some invention do as much to make this Thorn permanently an impressive object as the storm has made it to my eyes at this moment?' "

Wordsworth's Social Psychology: The Community of Natural Piety

A recent view of the characters in Wordsworth's poems contends that they do not belong, in their solitude and misery, to a community.[1] Because of his stress on the infinite and the unknown, Wordsworth is as far from a traditional sense of community—in the view of one scholar—as it is possible to be.[2]

Such a position is brought forward here because it seems to offer a good place to start an examination of Wordsworth's own views about the psychology of society; for a superficial reading of heavily anthologized poems might make the solitary, alien figure of some of those poems seem typical and make Wordsworth himself seem to be endorsing a view of a disjunctive, divisable society more in line with the radical social thinkers of his day, like Thomas Paine or William Godwin, whom he early admired. On the contrary, as we shall see, Wordsworth went even beyond Edmund Burke in his appeal to community.

Wordsworth's interest in society itself has never been questioned. The poet was clearly aware of such a penchant, perhaps even exaggerating its extent in a reported conversation of 1833: ". . . Although he was known to the world only as a poet, he had given," he claimed, "twelve hours thought to the condition and prospects of society, for one to poetry."[3] Lately Wordsworth has even been shown to have prefigured five specific sociological theories of Durkheim, Louis Wirth, and scholars of the Chicago School, although some of the resemblances seem far-fetched.[4] It is not, in any event, sociological phenomena that are of concern here, but rather the psychology of social relations.

Wordsworth's social psychology, as is so often the case, was connected with his political views, upon which a great deal of research has lately been expended.[5] His politics are now established as having been conservative at a very early date, and in fact very little of a revolutionary or even speculative nature can actually be found in his *published* work. Wordsworth did, of course, espouse radical causes after his return from France late in 1792; his "Letter to the Bishop of Llandaff" is the most obvious example, but, like further examples in the early versions of *Salisbury Plain*, it remained unpublished at the time. As Wordsworth tells us himself in *The Prelude*, he had been influenced by Michel Beaupuy and by conditions in France; these influences were thereupon reinforced and increased by his reading of French Ideologues and by his reading and acquaintance with William Godwin and English dissenters. And yet it is perhaps worth speculating that his radical politics were

sufficiently shortlived to be seen more as emotional out-
lets than as deep-seated, well-considered judgments.
Consider that for the last fifty-odd years of his life he
held what were clearly and consistently conservative, if
sometimes slightly maverick, views.

For at least by *Lyrical Ballads* (1798), or even earlier
by *The Borderers* (1797), Wordsworth's conservative bias
was already showing in a number of outcroppings,
probably under the influence of Edmund Burke.[6] Especially evident by 1798 is a more nearly sociological view,
even psychological—a view of the traditional community. The very idea of community has been seen by one
sociologist as of pivotal importance in the nineteenth
century and the quest for community as "the dominant
social tendency" of the twentieth.[7] Such a central interest on Wordsworth's part is perhaps partly what brought
Laura Wylie to claim that he was ahead of his time in his
concept of society.[8]

His social interests are largely psychological, shad-
ing off into what can only be called spiritual; the lines
are not always easily drawn. Wordsworth certainly
moved early from the abstractions of political science,
what he called the "general principles of the social order," to a view of society based on emotional and psychological bonds.[9] The community was seen as not
merely a group of people in a particular place, not a
mere collection of individuals anywhere,[10] and certainly
not, as Godwin and the other Radicals saw it, a group
that could be deliberately formed from the outside. A
community for Wordsworth was rather a state of mind
and feeling shared by a group who lived in a fixed locale
and whose bonds were the growth of many centuries.
Much later (1832), referring explicitly to Edmund

Burke, his mentor here, he wrote of "the vital power of social ties / Endeared by Custom."[11]

Wordsworth was interested in the psychological growth of these social ties, a growth which he epitomized as "Love of Nature Leading to Love of Mankind," the title of Book VIII of *The Prelude*. The necessity of such growth he spelled out in a fragment found in the Alfoxden Note-Book:

> And never for each other shall we feel
> As we may feel, till we have sympathy
> With nature in her forms inanimate. . . .[12]

There seems little doubt that Wordsworth believed the one love to be dependent on the other.[13]

The growth of this dependent human love is seen in *The Prelude* to run through stages. Of the generic "infant babe" he claims, "along his infant veins are interfused / The gravitation and the filial bond / Of Nature that connect him with the world" (1805; II, 262–64) or, as the Norton editors gloss the passage, "the 'filial bond' of child and mother . . . establishes the larger bond of man and Nature. . . ."[14] Sometime in late adolescence one can expect to experience the latter bond (or at least Wordsworth remembers having done so) as "A dawning, even as of another sense, / A human-heartedness about my love / For objects hitherto the gladsome air / Of my own private being, and no more . . ." (1805; IV, 224–227). And we are told in 1798 that "All things speak of man" to an adult, and again in 1841 that community with natural forms will lead him by their peace and love to "seek for objects of a kindred love / In fellow-natures and a kindred joy."[15]

In Book VIII of *The Prelude*, Wordsworth traces in

more detail the manner in which the growth of the love of man takes place under the influence of Nature. Natural surroundings—especially the more imposing and beautiful forms—provide the main incentive for human love: early on in life man is viewed "through objects that were great and fair" (1805; VIII, 451), even though love of Man must wait until late adolescence, "His hour," like Christ's at Canaan, "being not yet come" (1805; VIII, 490). Wordsworth, however, does go through considerable convolutions setting out his views.

Those views need not be true of Wordsworth in any detailed way, but they must be true of the generality of men in a general way, and so we become involved in the issue of the superiority of country life to city life, since nature is largely confined to the country. Wordsworth is theoretically committed to rejecting city life as devoid of those natural forms necessary for cultivating human love, and he does so commit himself, especially in Book VII of *The Prelude*, "Residence in London." But as Jonathan Wordsworth points out,[16] the narrator is ambivalent, finding pleasure in the city for much of the Book and only attacking it at the end:

> O, blank confusion, and a type not false
> Of what the mighty city is itself
> To all, except a straggler here and there—
> To the whole swarm of its inhabitants—
> An undistinguishable world to men,
> The slaves unrespited of low pursuits. . . .
>
> (1805; VII, 696–701)

It is true that there is ambivalence in the poet's approach to the city; he does find the city earlier in the Book "a vivid pleasure of my youth, and now, /

Among the lonely places that I love. . . ." (1805; VII,
151–52). He finds even the excitement of the city attrac-
tive, although it is usually its passive beauty that he ad-
mires; yet we needn't doubt the sincerity of his psychological theories when he finds himself called to feel
emotions despite those theories. We often like, after all,
what we know is not good for us.

The negative view of the city appears in *The Prelude*
almost immediately in his relief in the glad preamble of
Book I at escape from the city, and is in fact the other
side that Wordsworth felt just as strongly. In a letter of
1808, he deplores the lot of urban workers: "The mo-
notony of their employments renders some sort of stim-
ulus, intellectual or bodily, absolutely necessary for
them. Their work is carried on in clusters, Men from
different parts of the world, and perpetually changing;
so that every individual is constantly in the way of being
brought into contact with new notions and feelings, and
of being unsettled in his own accordingly."[17]

This position occurs so frequently that the end of
Book VII could hardly come "as a surprise," as one
scholar claims, although the vehemence of the attack on
London rises beyond the poet's usual tone.[18] And yet the
explanation for this charged emotion is easily explained.
Just as in the letter quoted above, the poet is dealing with
the effect on people of the anarchy and triviality of experience; and I think few things in life can be more
threatening than to have one's ability to order reality un-
dermined. This epistemological threat has been dealt
with ably by James Heffernan.[19]

Consequently, as the true love of man is largely the
property of rural man, so is the existence of true community largely rural; in fact the two concepts are
strongly interconnected. Whereas, "he by the vast me-

tropolis immured, / Where pity shrinks from unremitting calls, / Where numbers overwhelm humanity, / And neighborhood serves rather to divide / Than to unite," the rural society is:

> A true community—a genuine frame
> Of many into one incorporate.
> *That* must be looked for here; paternal sway,
> One household, under God, for high and low,
> One family and one mansion; to themselves
> Appropriate, and divided from the world. . . .
>
> (*Home at Grasmere*, 597–601, 615–20)

And the key to both concepts of community and of rural living is, I believe, "natural piety."

The words *pious* and *piety* have tended to lose part of their meaning in the past hundred years or so; oddly enough, despite the secularization which has more or less succeeded during the same time, piety has come to refer only to the observances owed to God. When, however, one reads Wordsworth's poetry, there are signs that the word meant something else as well both to him and to his contemporaries. In the sonnet, "Avaunt all Specious Pliancy of Mind," the poet used the expression "piety towards God," suggesting the existence of non-religious piety, an existence also suggested in a positive way by the title of another poem, "Filial Piety."

There was in fact a second current meaning of *piety* available to Wordsworth, one that went back to its Latin roots, *pius* and *pietas*. When Aeneas is called "pius Aeneas" at the beginning of the *Aeneid* it was not in recognition of his reverence for the gods, but rather of his reverence for his father, Anchises, whom he carried on his shoulders from burning Troy. There were thus two duties covered by the single word *pietas*: duty to the gods and duty to one's relatives, benefactors, country. This double function carried over into English, as a glance at Dr. Johnson's dictionary or the *O.E.D.* will substantiate.

The phrase "natural piety" occurs three times in Wordsworth's poetry, but never with a clear indication of the force of "natural." The phrase could signify a piety that's natural, perhaps inevitable, but only with the qualification that it not have been obstructed by urban life, and such is a large qualification. Or the phrase could mean, even less probably, a piety *toward* nature (a nod toward the religion of nature); but while Wordsworth did go through what is often called a pantheistic period, nature was seen even then as but a means toward something greater.

The phrase "natural piety" most likely was meant to convey the piety that lies on the human side (rather than the religious or "supernatural"), or so at least two of the usages suggest. One of these occurs in *The White Doe* (ll. 1231–32), where Francis Norton gave comfort to his captured father and brothers: "Tis well, for he the worst defied / Through force of natural piety. . . ." The second example (from "My Heart Leaps Up") is the best known:

> The Child is father of the Man;
> And I could wish my days to be
> Bound each to each by natural piety.

Here again there is a relational context of child and father, with the "natural" rather than the religious side of piety involved.

Perhaps, like the term *genial*, which links in one

word the concepts of joy and creativity, *piety* contains a fusion of its two meanings, the human and the divine, the psychological and the spiritual. Some usage seems to point in that direction. In the sonnet "I find it written of Simonides," Simonides buried a stranger, thus serving both man and the gods, who require the burial of all humans; his deed is termed simply "piety." The leech-gatherer in "Resolution and Independence" was also called *pious* in a letter Wordsworth wrote in 1802[20]; and he is described in the poem (1.98) in a dual function as one of those "who give to God and man their dues."

Piety of either kind, it should be clear, is not simply a legal or pro forma duty. In the *Essay on Epitaphs II,* Wordsworth seems to suggest a distinction between "dutiful children," those who follow the letter of the law, and "pious," those who are compelled by inner forces.[21] For piety is an emotional, even spiritual, bond between people, a familial and community relationship that depends on sharing place but that transcends the physical. In a larger context, piety is part of the poet's view of universal harmony and love, what he called in 1798 "one human heart" and later "the bond of brotherhood."[22]

The resulting view of the community of natural piety, this "true community," this "genuine frame / Of many into one incorporate" can be seen in action in many of the poems in *Lyrical Ballads,* but never more clearly than in remarks by Wordsworth on "The Idiot Boy" in a letter to John Wilson:

> . . . The loathing and disgust which many peo[ple] have at the sight of an Idiot, is a feeling which, though having som[e] foundation in human nature is not necessarily attached to it in any

vi[tal] degree, but is owing, in a great measure to a false delicacy, and, if I [may] say it without rudeness, a certain want of comprehensiveness of think[ing] and feeling. Persons in the lower classes of society have little or nothing [of] this: if an Idiot is born in a poor man's house it must be taken car[e of] and cannot be boarded out, as it would be by gentlefolks, or sent to [a] public or private receptacle for such unfortunate be[in]gs. Po[or people] seeing frequently among their neighbours such objects easily [dismiss what]ever there is of natural disgust about them, and have t[herefore] a sane state, so that without pain or suffering they [perform] their duties towards them.[23]

The phrase "poor people" is of course a reference to the poor cottagers of the Lake District, and their "duties" toward idiots are precisely part of the natural piety that validates their true community.

Wordsworth describes these cottagers in *A Guide to the Lake District* as "a perfect Republic of Shepherds and Agriculturists" and a "pure Commonwealth, the members of which existed in the midst of a powerful empire, like an ideal society or an organized community, whose constitution had been imposed and regulated by the mountains which protected it." In a note he added,

One of the most pleasing characteristics of manners in secluded and thinly-peopled districts, is a sense of the degree in which human happiness and comfort are dependent on the contingency of neighbourhood. This is implied by a rhyming adage common here, "*Friends are far, when neigh-*

bours are nar" (near). This mutual helpfulness is
not confined to out-of-doors work; but is ready
upon all occasions. Formerly, if a person became
sick, especially the mistress of a family, it was
usual for those of the neighbours who were more
particularly connected with the party by amica-
ble offices, to visit the house, carrying a present;
this practice, which is by no means obsolete, is
called *owning* the family, and is regarded as a
pledge of a disposition to be otherwise service-
able in a time of disability and distress.[24]

Writing a number of years before about the self-same
cottagers, Wordsworth addressed Charles James Fox, a
prominent whig politician who had earlier been allied to
Edmund Burke (but had split from him) and had, according to Wordsworth writing in 1818, been seduced
by the abstract rights of the French Revolution.[25] The
letter to Fox, which accompanied a presentation copy of
Lyrical Ballads (1800), is another important document
for understanding the community of natural piety. In it
the poet discusses "the bonds of domestic feeling among
the poor" of his district and their neighborly helpfulness. He offered "The Brothers" and "Michael" as two
poems about the "domestic affections"[26] and added:

The domestic affections will always be strong
amongst men who live in a country not crowded
with population, if these men are placed above
poverty. But if they are proprietors of small estates [as he had said they were], which have descended to them from their ancestors, the power
which these affections will acquire amongst such
men is inconceivable by those who have only had

an opportunity of observing hired labourers, farmers, and the manufacturing Poor. Their little tract of land serves as a kind of permanent rallying point for their domestic feelings, as a tablet upon which they are written which makes them objects of memory in a thousand instances when they would otherwise be forgotten. It is a fountain fitted to the nature of social man. . . .[27]

"This class of men," Wordsworth adds, "is rapidly disappearing."

That class of men, and indeed the true community, *were* fast eroding, until by the end of the century no one would be able to understand what Wordsworth was talking about, except by reports of those who had seen its final demise or by examination of what few vestiges remained.[28] Fortunately, one observer, George Sturt, far to the south of England, used such evidence to document in some detail a village community as it had existed in Bourne, near Farnham, Surrey.[29]

Life in Bourne in the late nineteenth century must have been very similar to that in Wordsworth's Lake District (and probably even up till about the same time); George Sturt continues to connect his cottagers to life in the eighteenth century.[30] Westmoreland cottagers were different from those in Bourne only in being literate in advance of the age and in owning small "estates." Otherwise, the resourcefulness, good-humored acceptance of things, and sheer endurance described in Sturt's book are clearly the same as those depicted in Wordsworth's poems.

More to the point, however, Sturt documents by anecdote and personal experience the "domestic affections" and especially the community spirit:

Before the property-owners came, and while still
the population was homogeneous, a sort of con-
tinuity in the life of the valley impressed itself
upon one's consciousness, giving a sense of se-
curity. Here amidst the heaths a laborious and
frugal people, wise in their own fashion, had
their home and supplied their own wants. Not
one of them probably thought of the significance
of it all, or understood how the village traditions
were his inheritance; not one considered what it
meant to him to belong to the little group of folk
and be independent of the whims of strangers.
Yet, for all that, there was comfort in the situation. To be so familiar as the people were with
the peculiarities of the valley, to appreciate the
usefulness of the wide heath-land, to value the
weather, to comprehend at a glance the doings of
the neighbors, and to have fellow-feeling with
their motives and hopes and disappointments,
was to be at home most intimately, most safely.
But all this is a thing of the past.[31]

After describing some of the ramifications of the disappearance of such a community, Sturt comments, "I shall
be told that, after all, this is mere sentiment. But, then,
half the comfort of life proceeds from those large vague
sentiments which lift a man's private doings up from
meanness into worthiness."[32] Could Wordsworth have
put it any better?

As Wordsworth continued to witness the dissolution
of the community, his concern continued as well. In late
spring of 1817, he wrote two letters expressing that concern:

. . . I see clearly that the principal ties which kept the different classes of society in a vital and harmonious dependence upon each other have, within these 30 years either been greatly impaired or wholly dissolved. Everything has been put up to market and sold for the highest price it would bring. Farmers used formerly to be attached to their Landlords, and labourers to their Farmers who employed them. All that kind of feeling has vanished—in like manner the connexion between the trading and landed interests of country towns undergoes no modification whatsoever from personal feeling, whereas within my memory it was almost wholly governed by it. . . . [Patronage at shops] was attended with substantial amity and interchanges of hospitality from generation to generation. All this moral cement is dissolved, habits and prejudices are broken and rooted up. . . .[33]

Notice the emphasis on ties, financial causes, the importance of feeling, and the generational connections. A month and a half later he brings up the same issues and concludes: "What loss has the country sustained within these last 20 or 30 years, of those habits, sentiments, and dispositions, which lend a collateral support, in the way of buttresses, of equal importance for the preservation of the edifice with the foundation itself?"[34] Within a year, his concern was so great—even to the point of fearing revolution—that he became active in Westmoreland politics. And twenty-six years later, in 1844, he was still anxious over the dissolution of the community.[35]

Wordsworth was perhaps too alarmed in 1817; at least, in the event, no revolution took place—most likely because of the series of political reforms that came in the late 1820's and 1830's. And Sturt makes a good case that there was something deep within the cottage community that kept it from serious discontent and political action.[36] Perhaps Wordsworth, despite his psychological probing of the community and his understanding of the community as a state of mind and feeling, had distanced himself in his lofty home at Rydal Mount and had sold his cottagers short. It could have been that like Edmund Burke before him he became alarmed at the breakdown of traditional social ties in the context of Revolution. 1817, the date of Wordsworth's letters, saw the passage of the Coercion Acts, and the Peterloo Massacre took place a mere two years later.

Some years earlier, the poet had a much higher opinion of, if not total confidence in, the community of natural piety. In "The Old Cumberland Beggar" (1798) we have a view of that community in action; by means of paradox, we see charity at work in a kind of bond or fellowship.[37] It is the nature of paradoxes that they most commonly turn on some little-considered spring in human nature, and like so many of Wordsworth's psychological poems "The Old Cumberland Beggar" has a paradox at its center.

Wordsworth not only tells us in the poem that beggars perform a function in binding together the community—as well as the past and present good deeds of its members—but he also implies that what the beggar thus provides is greater than what he receives:

> . . . Even such minds
> In childhood, from this solitary Being,
> Or from like wanderer, haply have received
> (A thing more precious far than all that books

Or the solicitudes of love can do!)
That first mild touch of sympathy and thought. . . .
(ll. 109–14)

And our cynical age, which especially suspects charitable motives that are not purely altruistic, is confronted by the claim that the villagers provide charity largely *for* that warm feeling that follows, "that after-joy / Which reason cherishes" (ll. 101–02).

To understand the full implications of Wordsworth's theme consider the modern equivalent of personal charity in the United States, The United Way, an organization that many American employees support by having a fixed amount of money automatically taken from their pay periodically. In this painless form of charity—in these "inevitable charities" as they become—the donor and receiver are as separate as it is possible to be. While the recipient is provided aid through an anonymous institution, the donor is not even aware of his donation beyond once signing a payroll card and cannot therefore receive anything from his own giving. His good deeds are bound together only by a computerized record, and the absence of any social, overall spiritual bonding is obvious. The jargon in a recent sociologist's view of the bond in "The Old Cumberland Beggar" as a "secular unintended mutually-maintaining social relationship" better describes such modern charity.[38]

Wordsworth's own behaviour towards beggars has been recorded in a letter by Ellis Yarnall. The event, which occurred in the last year of the poet's life, is illuminating in witnessing the long continuance of his earlier attitude:

We were standing together in the road, Wordsworth reading aloud, as I have said, when a man

> accosted us asking charity—a beggar of the better
> class. Wordsworth, scarcely looking off the
> book, thrust his hands into his pockets, as if in-
> stinctively acknowledging the man's right to beg
> by his prompt action. He seemed to find noth-
> ing, however; and he said, in a sort of soliloquy,
> "I have given to four or five, already, to-day," as
> if to account for his being then unprovided.[39]

The automatic, instinctual nature of the poet's response
is instructive in demonstrating his acceptance of his own
necessary piety as well as the rights of the beggar.

Wordsworth was also thereby witnessing his own
membership in a wider community of the District, not
perhaps as homogeneous nor spiritually close-knit a
community as the cottagers, but a community of natural piety nonetheless. The District was apparently unusual, if not unique, in its sense of larger community
beyond the cottagers; in the end of a description of
Wordsworth's seventy-fourth birthday party attended by
neighbors, and especially by children, of all classes,
Lady Richardson commented: "It is perhaps the only
part of the island where such a reunion of all classes
could have taken place without any connection of land-
lord and tenant, or any clerical relation, or school direction."[40] In a conversation recorded by his nephew,
Christopher, Wordsworth displayed his awareness of
such a community:

> Patriarchal usages have not quite deserted us of
> these valleys. This morning (new year's day) you
> were awakened early by the minstrels playing un-
> der the eaves, "Honour to Mr. Wordsworth!"
> "Honour to Mrs. Wordsworth!" and so to each

member of the household by name, servants included, each at his own window. These customs
bind us together as a family, and are as beneficial
as they are delightful. May they never disap-
pear![41]

Notice the mention of binding, generations, and the
metaphor of family for community.

These concepts occur frequently in the early poems,
especially the two—"The Brothers" and "Michael"—
singled out in the letter to Fox. As Michael Friedman
has pointed out, Wordsworth in "The Brothers" shows
us community responsibility, but there is more to the
poem than that, namely a larger spiritual dimension.[42]
Not only is there the question of absence of gravestones
(to be dealt with later), but after telling of Leonard's care
of his brother, the priest remarks that he had once said
"that God who made the great book of the world /
Would bless such piety" (ll. 266–67). Two bonds, however, had been broken, both of them bonds of natural
piety. One was the pious relation between the brothers,
for when Leonard had left and James

                              was left alone,
The little colour that he had was soon
Stolen from his cheek; he drooped, and pined, and
pined. . . .
                                        (ll. 338–40)

He even sought Leonard in his sleep—possibly thus being killed by a fall from a precipice. The other broken
bond was that linking Leonard to the community:

> For the boy loved the life which we lead here;
> And though of unripe years, a stripling only,
> His soul was knit to this his native soil.
>
> (ll. 296–98)

The community, the priest tells us, would welcome
Leonard back; that is not the problem. The narrator of
the poem lets us look into Leonard's soul, and we learn
that the bond has been snapped *within* him:

> . . . His long absence, cherished hopes,
> And thoughts which had been his an hour before,
> All pressed on him with such a weight, that now,
> This vale, where he had been so happy, seemed
> A place in which he could not bear to live. . . .
>
> (ll. 422–26)

And so he left the community of natural piety for good.

In "Michael," the other poem recommended to Fox,
there are the same bonds, the "links of love" (l.401) between Michael and Luke,as well as the feeling of community (l.428–30). There is also a similar breaking away
of a family member from the community of natural
piety (again with the best of motives), as well as a consequent deterioration. But "Michael" conveys a major
principle hardly touched upon in "The Brothers," the
role of land ownership in domestic and community affections:

> Their little tract of land serves as a kind of per-
> manent rallying point for their domestic feelings,
> as a tablet upon which they are written which
> makes them objects of memory in a thousand in-
> stances when they would otherwise be forgotten.

It is a fountain fitted to the nature of social man
from which supplies of affection, as pure as his
heart was intended for, are daily drawn.[43]

This same passage in the letter to Fox provides the
necessary gloss for understanding another early poem
concerning the psychology of the domestic affections,
"The Last of the Flock." It is a difficult poem, for the
shepherd's inability to love his children after losing most
of the property he had taken so long to accumulate
might seem to put him in a bad light. And yet there is
nothing in the treatment of the shepherd to suggest that
Wordsworth sees him as guilty of wrong feelings. Jonathan Wordsworth also reads the poem in this way, but
sees the disabled affections as due to a failure of what he
calls elsewhere "the general harmony of existence,"[44]
whereas I would think his disability derives more strictly
from the "fountain" of property (in this case on the
hoof) having been dried up and with it, in reverse of the
quotation above, the affections which it supplies.

In any event, the psychology underlying the affective
disorder is clear enough to us today, having witnessed
innumerable times the effects of unemployment on
men. The economic repercussions have been at least
softened by social welfare programs, but nothing has
been developed to cope with the emotional trauma—the
failure of self-respect, the frustration, and the breakdown of family. Moral breakdown and paranoia ensue
for the shepherd:

> "To wicked deeds I was inclined,
> And wicked fancies crossed my mind;
> And every man I chanced to see,
> I thought he knew some ill of me. . . ."
>
> (ll. 71–74)

Even the dilemma of the welfare agency is faced, with the victim as yet only half-destitute:

> ". . . How can we give to you,"
> They cried, "what to the poor is due?"
>
> (ll.49–50)

Again the tone does not suggest that they are wrong either, for with a sizeable flock, the shepherd is in fact well off still.

And so he must be brought to his knees. The same sort of study occurs in the Story of Margaret (*The Ruined Cottage*) in Book I of *The Excursion*, in which Robert succumbs to the psychological consequences of unemployment, after several seasons of drought:

> "A sad reverse it was for him who long
> Had filled with plenty, and possessed in place,
> This lonely Cottage. At the door he stood,
> And whistled many a snatch of merry tunes
> That had no mirth in them. . . ."
>
> (ll. 566–70)

Then, "not less idly," he did odd jobs of maintenance:

> "But this endured not; his good humour soon
> Became a weight in which no pleasure was:
> And poverty brought on a petted mood
> And a sore temper: day by day he drooped. . . ."
>
> (ll. 578–81)

Finally, after wandering about listlessly, he too found his domestic affections eroded:

"One while he would speak lightly of his babes,
And with a cruel tongue: at other times
He tossed them with a false unnatural joy:
And 'twas a rueful thing to see the looks
Of the poor innocent children."

(ll. 585–89)

Following the tradition of Arnold's "Wragg in custody," a short item appeared in a recent newspaper on the back page (italics added):

Swift action by two policemen may have saved the life of two-year-old Carol Hicks, found stabbed in the heart yesterday. Her injured sister Sandra, three, lay beside her, and the body of their father was found nearby.

. . . .

Their father, John Hicks, 31, *unemployed*, was discovered dead in an outhouse. Detectives are satisfied nobody else was involved.

Avoiding such extremes, the unemployed Robert (in the Story of Margaret) merely enlists and leaves for foreign parts; but the potential for worse is conveyed in Wordsworth's lines; for consider what might have happened, with his mind becoming more and more unhinged, if the relief of enlistment had not been available. Margaret, his wife, once the family is fragmented, begins a gradual decline that causes the death of one child (by neglect) and demonstrates the same deterioration affecting the female psyche.

Necessity brought on by poverty produces another example of natural piety on the positive side, the treatment of idiots by their families. In the letter of 1802 to John Wilson defending his poem "The Idiot Boy," Wordsworth abjures the squeamishness of the upper classes toward idiocy:

> Po[or people] seeing frequently among their neighbours such objects, easily [dismiss what]ever there is of natural disgust about them, and have t[herefore] a sane state, so that without pain or suffering they [perform] their duties towards them.[45]

Wordsworth considered such "duties" (or pieties) of parents "the great triumph of the human heart."[46]

But the community of natural piety may extend beyond the human heart, or at least a good many poems suggest as much, even though the ideas conveyed may seem conventional on the surface. Sufficient instances of natural piety in animals, of bonds between creatures, accumulate to make a case.

In "Hart-leap Well," for example, a knight kills a hart for mere sport (the animal is left where killed); and not only does nature curse the spot with withered trees, but we are told of the spring at the death-spot:

> "There's neither dog nor heifer, horse nor sheep,
> Will wet his lips within that cup of stone. . . ."
> (ll. 133–34)

The bonds broken even go beyond the animal community, for "some say that here a murder has been done . . ." (line 137), and the hart is given human characteristics:

> . . . We cannot tell
> What cause the Hart might have to love this place,
> And come and make his death-bed near the well.
>
> (ll. 146–48)

And a further spiritual dimension is added (ll. 163–68):

> . . . This Beast not unobserved by Nature fell;
> His death was mourned by sympathy divine.
>
> The Being, that is in the clouds and air,
> That is in the green leaves among the groves,
> Maintains a deep and reverential care
> For the unoffending creatures whom he loves.

As in "Tintern Abbey," the pantheism of the middle lines above shades off into a more orthodox personal God, who sympathizes, cares, and loves, and who is part of what could be called the Cosmic Community. The two kinds of piety merge again.

Sometimes the bonds seem more conventional, namely between animals and humans—the bonds joining them into one community. In *The Waggoner* the central "human element" in the poem that gives it warmth and humor is the love of the horses for Benjamin. The horses are given more than animal understanding; when the alcoholic Benjamin stops for the fatal drink, they "halted, though reluctantly" (II, 51), and after his drinking, they have no "disheartening doubts and dread," for they know

> That Benjamin, with clouded brains,
> Is worth the best with all their pains;
> And, if they had a prayer to make,

The prayer would be that they may take
With him whatever comes in course,
The better fortune or the worse. . . .

                                        (III, 12–18)

Notice that the question posed is not whether they *can* pray but whether they do so. Aware of the stakes involved (IV, 88–94), they attempt to make up the time lost, and when they fail to and Benjamin is fired, they will work for no one else. Such animal devotion occurs in many other poems, most notably in the behavior of the ass in *Peter Bell*.

Even the water of the spring in "Hart-leap Well" is involved in the response to the "murder" by sending "forth a dolorous groan" (line 136). For if animals seem to be entering the membership of the human community, inanimate creation tends to take on the life and sensation of the animal community. Such a view is known as animism, and it is said to have come to Wordsworth through Darwin, Priestley, and others; but Darwin, at least, was concerned with vegetable phenomena like the Venus Fly Trap, while Wordsworth has something less conventional in mind.[47] Presumably from fear of seeming extravagant, Wordsworth is not forthright in presenting his views, which often seem like metaphor or pathetic fallacy, and are often taken as such. But there are too many examples to dismiss the concept itself so easily.

It first occurs in a passage to the revised, unpublished version of *An Evening Walk*, said to have been composed in 1794:[48]

A heart that vibrates evermore, awake
To feeling for all forms that Life can take,

That wider still its sympathy extends
And sees not any line where being ends;
Sees sense, through Nature's rudest forms betrayed,
Tremble obscure in fountain rock and shade,
And while a secret power those forms endears
Their social accents never vainly hears.

The statement about "being" (line 4) is ambiguous; "being" is apparently meant to be synonymous with "life" (line 2), but the last four lines clearly convey that fountains, rocks, and trees possess "sense" and "social accents," presumably a reaching into community.

The social aspects of animism recur in fragments written in the Alfoxden Notebook (compiled probably between January and 19 March 1798):

And never for each other should we feel
As we may feel, till we have sympathy
With nature in her forms inanimate,
With objects such as have no power to hold
Articulate language. In all forms of things
There is a mind.

(*PW*, V, 340)

This passage is similar to the previous quotation in that the animism is likewise unqualified, but the passages were both unpublished. In the future, such instances of animism would be published and qualified either explicitly or through inherent ambiguity.

"Lines Written in Early Spring," composed probably just after the above fragment, contains perhaps the most insistent testimonies to animism, beginning with a mention of bonds between the narrator and inanimate nature (1798 version): "To her fair works did nature link

/ The human soul that through me ran" (ll. 5–6). The next three stanzas argue strongly:

> Through primrose-tufts, in that sweet bower,
> The periwinkle trail'd its wreaths;
> And 'tis my faith that every flower
> Enjoys the air it breathes.
>
> The birds around me hopp'd and play'd:
> Their thoughts I cannot measure,
> But the least notion which they made,
> It seem'd a thrill of pleasure.
>
> The budding twigs spread out their fan,
> To catch the breezy air;
> And I must think, do all I can,
> That there is pleasure there.

Wordsworth seems to be clearly positing a serious belief in the sensibility of plants and birds that "link" themselves to the human in a kind of community, and yet the qualifiers in the passage ("'Tis my faith," "It seemed," and "I must think, do all I can"), followed by two "ifs" in the last stanza (not quoted above), have caused the animism to be taken figuratively or at any rate not seriously.

From about the same period (early 1798) come lines 448–51 of the two-part *Prelude*:

> I was only then
> Contented when with bliss ineffable
> I felt the sentiment of being spread
> O'er all that moves, and all that seemeth still. . . .[49]

The speaker includes all animals and even the inanimate
waves and "depth of waters" themselves, adding a new
spiritual dimension only hinted at before:

> Wonder not
> If such my transports were, for in all things
> I saw one life, and felt that it was joy. . . .

But then he draws back in a feint of orthodoxy: "If this
be error, and another faith / Find easier access to the
pious mind. . . ."[50]
Another instance of how deeply animism appealed
to Wordsworth occurs in a letter to Coleridge late the
next year (1799): "Besides, am I fanciful when I would
extend the obligation of gratitude to insensate things?
May not a man have a salutary pleasure in doing something gratuitously for the sake of his house, as for an
individual to which he owes so much."[51] The interrog-
atory form and the parenthetical nature of the remark
make it seem less serious than it otherwise might be
taken.
The spiritual dimension continued as "an *active* Principle," at the opening of Book IX (composed in 1798)
of *The Excursion*, "that subsisted in all things, in all nature," in stars, clouds, flowers, trees, stones, rocks, water, and air. It later showed up in Book III (1805), lines
121–27, of *The Prelude*, composed in 1804 and heavily
qualified:

> A track pursuing not untrod before,
> From deep analogies by thought supplied
> Or consciousness not to be subdued,
> To every natural form, rock, fruit or flower,
> Even the loose stones that cover the highway,

I gave a moral life—I saw them feel,
Or linked them to some feeling.

The first "or" clause adds more to the animistic belief
while the second undercuts it altogether.

Discussions of Wordsworth's animism usually end
with the early *Prelude*, but animism continued at least
into the 1820's. In his "Address to Kilchurn Castle,"
composed between 1820 and 1827, there is a short passage reminiscent of earlier statements:

Oh! there is life that breathes not; Powers there are
That touch each other to the quick in modes
Which the gross world no sense hath to perceive,
No soul to dream of.

                                          (ll. 6–9)

And as late as 1829, the speaker in "Humanity" describes the passing of the use of "Rocking-stones" for
"judicial and religious purposes" and then comments:

Yet, for the Initiate, rocks and whispering trees
Do still perform mysterious offices!
And functions dwell in beast and bird that sway
The reasoning mind, or with the fancy play,
Inviting, at all seasons, ears and eyes
To watch for undelusive auguries:—
Not uninspired appear their simplest ways;
Their voices mount symbolical of praise—
To mix with hymns that Spirits make and hear;
And to fallen man their innocence is dear.

                                          (ll. 9–18)

Here the animism is laced with suggestions of a kind of religious community, uniting rocks, trees, beasts, birds, Spirits, fallen man, and God.

But the mention of "Spirits" may portend an even wider human community that extends beyond the grave. Like the extension among animals and inanimate objects, this widening can be seen in a number of poems and is usually taken as an exercise in poetic license rather than as a considered belief of the poet. In any event, the divisions between life and death are often blurred; the speaker in "Maternal Grief" exclaims:

> Death, life, and sleep, reality and thought,
> Assist me, God, their boundaries to know. . . .
> (ll. 11–12)

And, indeed, such help would often be useful in reading Wordsworth's poetry.

For example, there is a passage deleted from the "Intimations Ode" after 1815:

> To whom the grave
> Is but a lonely bed without the sense or sight
> Of day or the warm light,
> A place of thought where we in waiting lie.

Perhaps a background note to this passage should be taken from Dorothy Wordsworth's *Journal* of 29 April 1802, a date which fell during the composition of the poem: "We then went to John's Grove, sate a while at first. Afterwards William lay, and I lay in the trench under the fence. . . . He thought that it would be as sweet thus to lie so in the grave, to hear the *peaceful* sounds of the earth, and just to know that our dear friends were near."⁵² Coleridge, who apparently did not share this belief, objected in the *Biographia Literaria* to the "frightful notion of lying *awake* in his grave."⁵³

"Peaceful," the word underscored by Dorothy, describes part of the attraction of death, which can perhaps be seen as the ultimate passivity. It is at least a kind of peace that goes far beyond what that state usually conveys. In "Glen-Almain," celebrating the glen that was thought to contain the grave of Ossian, we are told of "calm; there cannot be / A more entire tranquility" and of "perfect rest":

> A convent, even a hermit's cell,
> Would break the silence of this Dell:
> It is not quiet, is not ease;
> But something deeper far than these:
> The separation that is here
> Is of the grave; and of austere
> Yet happy feelings of the dead. . . .
>
> (ll. 23–29)

And in "Elegiac Stanzas Composed in the Churchyard of Grasmere," the same extraordinary state exists:

> Now do those sternly-featured hills
> Look gently on this grave;
> And quiet *now* are the depths of air,
> As a sea without a wave.
>
> But deeper lies the heart of peace
> In quiet more profound;
> The heart of quietness is here
> Within this churchyard bound.
>
> (ll. 17–24)

But beyond this epiphenomenal peacefulness, there is also the attraction of communal bonds bridging what most see as a wide abyss. In *The Essay on Epitaphs* Wordsworth writes both of "a community of the living and the dead" and of a "Communion between living and dead"; in *The Convention of Cintra* pamphlet he writes of "a spiritual community binding together the living and the dead"; and in a letter of 5 January 1813, Dorothy mentions "that bond betwixt the living and the dead."[54]

Within such a context we are not unduly surprised to read in "The Brothers" that

> "The thought of death sits easy on the man
> Who has been born and dies among the mountains."
> (ll. 182–83)

Nor will we be surprised to find that no gravestones are used in the community of natural piety:

> "In our church-yard
> Is neither epitaph nor monument,
> Tombstone nor name—only the turf we tread
> And a few natural graves."
> (ll. 12–15)

For here, in one of the few surviving communities in England,

> "We have no need of names and epitaphs;
> We talk about the dead by our fire-sides."
> (ll. 178–79)

One of the two other instances of the absence of gravestones occurs in the same district and for the same reason (*Excursion*, VI, 610–12):

>   These Dalesmen trust
> The lingering gleam of their departed lives
> To oral record, and the silent heart. . . .

In the other case, where brave warriors have fallen anonymously and "lie / In the blank earth," there is no question of community bonds leaving them without a stone, and yet the extended community is nevertheless involved (*The River Duddon*, XXIX):

> The passing Winds memorial tribute pay;
> The Torrents chant their praise. . . .

In all these instances, without tombstones and with remembrance instead coming from within the communities, the boundary between life and death seems less certain.

In their own lives, William and Dorothy seemed to have shared the view of a community overlapping life and death, and there was opportunity enough in the death of their brother John (1805) and two of William's children (1812). Of his brother, Wordsworth said: "I shall never forget him, never lose sight of him, there is a bond between us yet, the same as if he were living, nay far more sacred. . . ."[55] Dorothy was convinced her dead brother would not be gone: "I shall have him with me."[56] ". . . Our dear brother, who though taken from our earthly sight is for ever with us and will be so to our dying day. . . ."[57] ". . . His exalted Nature has not perished—but Oh! far better—and we who remain on earth shall have him with us, a perpetual presence."[58] At one point, she makes the odd admission: "I had even a feeling of *joy* the first time I heard the wind in my bed after we heard the tidings—but why dwell upon these things?" The self-interruption might well suggest an awareness of sailing in very unconventional waters.[59]

In 1812, Thomas and Catherine, two Wordsworth children, died. Amid some very conventional remarks, Dorothy made some ambiguous statements about Thomas:

> The image of him, his very self, is so vivid in my mind—it is with me like a perpetual presence. . . . At times, when I muse on a future life and on his blessedness in another world, I lose those thoughts of anguish; the child becomes spiritualized to my mind. I wish I could have such musings more frequently—and longer; but alas! the image of the Boy disturbs me—and I weep again.[60]

Several months later, after the move to Rydal Mount, she remarks, "The weather is delightful, and the place a paradise; but my inner thoughts *will* go back to Grasmere. I was the last person who left the House yesterday evening. It seemed as quiet as the grave; and the very church-yard where our darlings lie, when I gave a last look upon it [seemed] to chear my thoughts."[61] And of Thomas a few months later, she wrote: "I see him wherever I turn."[62] Wordsworth himself was much more orthodox in his comments at the time, and yet four years later he remarks: "This was four years ago—but they are perpetually present to my eyes—I do not mourn for them; yet I am sometimes weak enough to wish that I had them again."[63] It is not clear whether in all these instances Dorothy and William are merely exaggerating in their grief; in the context of their past beliefs, there seems to be more in these statements than that, especially in the constant references to *seeing* those who have passed beyond what is normally considered the boundary of death.

Childhood for Wordsworth was a special time of life in which everyone seems to share the myopia towards death. According to the "Intimations Ode," it is a time when the rational faculty has not yet become dominant and so the mind is less likely to set up or accept the boundaries we seem to need to lead normal lives. Wordsworth brought his own life forward in several places as evidence for the disbelief of the child in death: "At that time I could not believe that I should lie down quietly in the grave, and that my body would moulder into dust."[64] In a letter, he argued that the Ode was based on two "recollections of childhood," one of which was "an indisposition to bend to the law of death as applying to our particular case."[65] In the note to the poem dictated to Isabella Fenwick, he repeats the last point and adds that as a child he believed he could be apotheosized into heaven.[66]

In all three quotations, there is a note of resistance and individual involvement, which is perhaps misleading, certainly with reference to the ode. It is as if death had offered a personal affront to the child's ego, and this attitude is missing from the adult view of William and Dorothy and from other instances in the poems involving children. In the most famous poem dealing with the subject, "We are Seven," it is rather a question of understanding:

—A simple Child
That lightly draws its breath,
And feels its life in every limb,
What should it know of death?

The narrator of the poem continues by telling of a conversation with a little girl whose sister and brother are buried in a nearby churchyard but are not to be therefore discounted as members of her family. While conversing, he won't say directly what is on his mind, but simply counts the child's living siblings and omits the dead ones:

"You say that two at Conway dwell,
And two are gone to sea,
Yet ye are seven! I pray you tell,
Sweet Maid, how this may be."

(ll. 25–28)

The maid repeats her list and includes the two " 'in the church-yard,' " and, on being finally told that they don't count, insists on the factual nature of their existence (" 'Their graves are green, they may be seen' ") before simply assuming that death does not signify division. Like the two who " 'are gone to sea' " (line 20), Jane " 'went away' " (having " 'died' ") and John " 'was forced to go.' " The use of the verb *to go* is not strictly speaking a euphemism, like the narrator's " 'they two are in heaven,' " but rather seems to be her way of conveying the absence of this boundary in her view of things. She has no special insight; rather (which may amount to the same thing) she *lacks* a notion of boundary, a limit to community. As Alan Bewell argues, the girl feels "that death is not radically discontinuous with life and that death is "a communal state.""[67]

Some fourteen years after the composition of the poem, the Wordsworths were living in the Rectory, Grasmere, and their own children played in the grave-yard across the road.[68] After the death of Catherine in 1812, Dorothy reported in a letter that the eight-year-old Dora

> was at Appleby—she was always particularly fond of Catherine, and when she heard of her death was much afflicted for a time; but she is of a volatile nature, and the next day was as happy as ever. She came home last Thursday and we were surprized at her joyfulness, but at night when she went to bed she knelt down before me to say her prayers, and as usual prayed for her Brothers and sister, I suppose without thinking of her.[69]

Dorothy thereupon reenacted the next stage in the story of "We are Seven," playing the emotional bully with somewhat the same results:

> I said to her when she had done—My dear child you have no Sister living now—and our Religion does not teach us to pray for the dead. We can do nothing for them—our prayers will not help them—God has taken your Sister to himself.— She burst into a flood—an agony of tears—and went weeping and silent to her bed—and I left her after some time still weeping—and so she fell asleep.

In this extraordinary instance of life imitating art, there is a kind of verification of the art, for Dora's weeping and eventual silence is but another form of the denial conveyed in the poem by simple repetition of statement.

The series of early poems known as "the Lucy poems" also often suggest an absence of demarcation between life and death; and placing them in this context can make the meaning of those often obscure poems a little clearer. In "A Slumber Did My Spirit Seal," if the "spirit" in the first line is identical to the "she" in the third, we could simply have another instance of the breakdown of distinctions:

> A slumber did my spirit seal;
> I had no human fears:
> She seemed a thing that could not feel
> The touch of earthly years.

Indeed, why should the speaker have "fears," when "she" could as well be asleep and *seems* beyond death; likewise in the second stanza we are not told that she is dead, but rather that she has no "motion," "force," hearing, nor vision, but is part of a larger community of "rocks, and stones, and trees." As Alan Bewell insists, the speaker is "unable to discriminate living from inanimate things . . . ."[70]

In "Three Years She Grew in Sun and Shower," Nature decides to " 'take' " the three-year-old Lucy into the same larger community:

> "And hers shall be the breathing balm,
> And hers the silence and the calm
> Of mute insensate things."

She joins the clouds, willows, storms, stars, and rivulets, as we are told in Nature's soliloquy. The narrator then tells us Lucy "died" and left him with a "memory of what has been, / And never more will be." Such, however, is *his* view, not the correct view of Nature.

Of all the Lucy poems, "I Travelled Among Unknown Men" is the most conventional and easily understood, even though the death of Lucy is conveyed in a round-about way:

> And thine too is the last green field
> That Lucy's eyes surveyed.

"She Dwelt among the Untrodden Ways" is likewise more easily understood, but the last stanza is worth scrutiny:

> She lived unknown, and few could know
>   When Lucy ceased to be;
> But she is in her grave, and, oh,
>   The difference to me!

Again you have circumlocutions—not euphemisms— for "die" ("ceased to be" and "is in her grave") and again the speaker gives *his* view, which need not be the poet's.

In "Lucy Gray," which is not one of the "Lucy poems," there is another clearer case of blurring the division between life and death. Lucy Gray, a young girl lost in a storm, is traced to the middle of a bridge where her footprints stop, but the local community are not all convinced about the boundaries of that community:

> —Yet some maintain that to this day
> She is a living child;

> That you may see sweet Lucy Gray
> Upon the lonesome wild.

And the narrator, himself apparently unconvinced, adds:

> O'er rough and smooth she trips along,
> And never looks behind;
> And sings a solitary song
> That whistles in the wind.

It may be that what they *see* is Lucy's ghost, but such a reading is unnecessary, as we have seen.[71]

For Wordsworth's view of the mind at work in society crosses other lines, political, social, but especially mystical. To Coleridge as well as to himself, "The unity of all [had] been revealed," and that unity shows up concretely in Wordsworth's social psychology. In the same passage in *The Prelude* (1805; II, 220–24), he addresses Coleridge:

> Thou art no slave
> Of that false secondary power by which
> In weakness we create distinctions, then
> Deem that our puny boundaries are things
> Which we perceive, and not which we have made.

Wordsworth was concerned to dissolve such boundaries created between the inanimate and animate, the animal and human, and finally between the living and the dead. These boundaries are not necessarily perceived but might have been created by the human mind as a way of keeping things orderly. In the process, moreover, humanity has lost the sense of community—not only the community between men, fast disappearing from the Lake District, but in its wider aspects—a spiritual community which Wordsworth had himself perceived.

NOTES

1. John P. Ward, *Poetry and the Sociological Idea* (London, 1981), pp. 116–118. Herbert Lindenberger in Chapter 7 of *On Wordsworth's Prelude* (Princeton, 1963), argues that Wordsworth's central characters are solitaries who are shadowy and unreal.
2. Ward, p.117: Wordsworth's characters miss "kinship and residence" and there seems "something wrong ...with humanity specifically in its communal aspects."
3. Rev. Orville Dewey, *The Old World and the New* (New York, 1836), I, 90. The date of the remark was July 30, 1833.
4. John P. Ward, "Wordsworth and the Sociological Idea," *Critical Quarterly*, 16 (1974), 335–50.
5. See F. M. Todd, *Politics and the Poet: A Study of Wordsworth* (London, 1957); Leslie F. Chard II, *Dissenting Republican: Wordsworth's Early Life and Thought in Their Political Context* (The Hague, 1972); James K. Chandler, *Wordsworth's Second Nature: A Study of the Poetry and Politics* (Chicago, 1984).
6. Chandler, Chapter 3.
7. Robert A. Nisbet, *The Sociological Tradition* (London, 1967), p. 47; *The Quest for Community* (New York, 1953), p. 45.
8. Laura J. Wylie, *Social Studies in English Literature* (Boston and New York, 1916), p. 134.
9. Ernest de Selincourt, ed., *The Letters of William and Dorothy Wordsworth: The Early Years*, second edition, revised by Chester L. Shaver (Oxford, 1967), I, 124. Hereafter cited as *Letters: Early Years*.
10. For a definition of community, see David W. Minor and Scott Greer, eds., *The Concept of Community* (London, 1970), intro, p. ix.
11. Jonathan Wordsworth et al, eds., *William Wordsworth: The Prelude* (New York and London, 1979), p. 255. (1850 version, VII, 527–28. Quotations from *The Prelude* will be taken from this edition and will hereafter be cited in the text only as to version, book, and line,)
12. Ernest de Selincourt and Helen Darbishire, eds., *The Poetical Works*

of William Wordsworth (Oxford, 1949), V, 340. Hereafter cited in text as *PW*.

13. Jonathan Wordsworth has in fact argued (in *William Wordsworth: The Borders of Vision* [Oxford, 1982], p.285) that the causal connection between love of nature and man, especially as set forth in Book VIII, was forced by the poet and that he had little fellow-feeling at the time of writing. The argument derives from the very careful dating of manuscripts combined with an assumption that the poem is strictly autobiographical, a combination that easily leads to some predictable problems. At one place, for example, the causal connection between the two loves is described as "a long way in Wordsworth's past" and then two sentences later we are told (p. 288) that "he even towards the end of Book VIII recollects the belief of 1798," the very causal connection dismissed above. The passage used to demonstrate the poet's distance from love of men in 1804, moreover, is not continued far enough by Jonathan Wordsworth, for the passage in question is referred to ten lines later:

> Yet who can tell while he this path
> Hath been ascending, in *apparent* slight
> Of men and all the mild humanities. . . . (italics added)

This is followed by a reiteration of how the love of nature leads to love of man. Jonathan Wordsworth is correct in his criticism of the presentation of the causal connection between love of man and nature in Book VIII; it is, as I have said, not well argued by the poet, but it is supported by passages elsewhere, and, more importantly, it is not worthwhile to treat *The Prelude* as a treatise in philosophy or in psychology. It is preeminently a poem and, as poetry, conveys what the poet wishes to convey about the love of man.

Although Jonathan Wordsworth does not mention it, the claim that Wordsworth had difficulty sympathizing with man has a long tradition; see Lindenberger, pp. 205–06. See also James Scoggins, *Imagination and Fancy* (Lincoln, Nebraska, 1966), pp. 220–21.

14. Jonathan Wordsworth et al, p. 78n.
15. *The Excursion*, IV, 1239, 1216–17.
16. Jonathan Wordsworth, *William Wordsworth: The Borders of Vision* (Oxford, 1982), pp. 295, 305.
17. Ernest de Selincourt, *The Letters of William and Dorothy Wordsworth: The Middle Years, Part I*, second edition, revised Mary Moorman (Oxford, 1969), II, 248–49. Hereafter cited as *Letters: Middle Years, Part I*. Edward J. Ahearn ("The Search for Community: the City

in Holderin, Wordsworth and Baudelaire," *Texas Studies in Language and Literature*, 13 [1971], 80–81) claims that Wordsworth illuminates the alienation of man in the modern city.

18. Jonathan Wordsworth, *Borders*, p. 304.

19. James A. W. Heffernan, *Wordsworth's Theory of Poetry: The Transforming Imagination* (Ithaca, 1969), Chapter 5.

20. *Letters: The Early Years*, I, 367 (W. W. to Sara Hutchinson, 14 June 1802): "But Good God! Such a figure, in such a place, a pious self-respecting, miserably infirm, and [ ] Old Man telling such a tale!"

21. W. J. B. Owen and Jane W. Smyser, *The Prose Works of William Wordsworth*, II, 63–69. Hereafter cited as *Prose Works*.

22. "The Old Cumberland Beggar," line 153; *The Excursion*, II, 562.

23. John O. Hayden, "Wordsworth's Letter to John Wilson (1802): A Corrected Version," *The Wordsworth Circle*, 18 (1987), 37.

24. "Guide," *Prose Works*, II, 206.

25. "Two Addresses," *Prose Works*, III, 157.

26. The "domestic affections" are also discussed in "A Guide through the District of the Lakes," *Prose Works*, II, 312.

27. *Letters: The Early Years*, I, 314–15.

28. For the destruction of the agricultural village community, see Minor and Greer, p. xi. Alan Bewell, in his *Wordsworth and the Enlightenment* (New Haven, 1989), even claims Wordsworth in his poetry sought "to give a 'substance and life' to a specific way of life that he knew was disappearing" (p. 31). The claim of the existence of such a "project" is not supported by evidence.

29. George Sturt (pseud. George Bourne), *Change in the Village* (London, 1912).

30. Sturt, pp. 115, 125.

31. Sturt, pp. 181–82.

32. Sturt, p. 182.

33. Ernest de Selincourt, *The Letters of William and Dorothy Wordsworth: The Middle Years, Part II*, second edition, revised Mary Moorman and Alan G. Hill (Oxford, 1970), III, 375–76. This volume will be cited hereafter as *Letters: The Middle Years, Part II*.

34. *Letters: The Middle Years, Part II*, III, 388.

35. Ernest de Selincourt, ed., *The Letters of William and Dorothy Wordworth*, second edition, rev. by Alan G. Hill (Oxford, 1988), VII, 561.

36. Sturt, Chapter VII.

37. Two recent views of the poem seem to me to miss its main point. James H. Averill (*Wordsworth and the Poetry of Human Suffering* [Ith-

aca, N.Y., 1980], p.120) claims the poem is "about the imagination's relation to suffering." James K. Chandler (*Wordsworth's Second Nature* [Chicago, 1984], p.89) is closer to the truth, but still off the point, with his claim that natural manners is "the real topic" of the poem.

38. Ward, "Wordsworth and the Sociological Idea," p. 339.
39. A. B. Grosart, ed., *The Prose Works of William Wordsworth* (London, 1896), III, 483.
40. Grosart, III, 444. George Sturt throughout his *Change in the Village* cited above, documents how his cottage community is cut off from any larger community, as indeed it must have been by 1911.
41. Grosart, III, 464.
42. Michael H. Friedman, *The Making of a Tory Humanist* (New York, 1979), p.180.
43. *Letters: The Early Years*, I, 314–15.
44. Jonathan Wordsworth, *The Music of Humanity*, pp. 247, 248–49.
45. Hayden, "Wordsworth's Letter," p. 37.
46. Hayden, "Wordsworth's Letter," p. 37.
47. Herbert W. Piper, *The Active Universe* (London, 1962), pp. 27, 69.
48. I believe the passage was added a few years later, probably in 1798 but possibly even as late as 1820. See John Hayden, "The Dating of the '1794' Version of Wordsworth's *An Evening Walk*," *Studies in Bibliography*, 42 (1989), 265–71. See *PW*, I, 10n.
49. Jonathan Wordsworth et al, p. 25.
50. In Book III (1805), 121–126, occurs another passage:

> A track pursuing not untrod before,
> From deep analogies by thought supplied,
> Or consciousness not to be subdued,
> To every natural form, rock, fruit or flower,
> Even the loose stones that cover the highway,
> I gave a moral life—I saw them feel,
> Or linked them to some feeling.

The two qualifications, one preceding, one following "or," make the assertion seem less certain, as usual.

51. *Letters: The Early Years*, I, 275.
52. Mary Moorman, ed., *The Journals of Dorothy Wordsworth* (Oxford, 1971), p.117. See also *The Excursion*, IV, 237–38, "'rejoicing secretly / In the sublime attractions of the grave' "; for Wordsworth's high opinion of the passage see *Letters: The Middle Years*, III, 190–91.

53. James Engell and W. Jackson Bate, eds., *Biographia Literaria* (Princeton, NJ, 1983), II, 141.
54. Owen and Smyser, II, 56, 66; I, 339; *Letters: The Middle Years*, III, 61.
55. *Letters: The Early Years*, I, 547.
56. *Letters: The Early Years*, I, 559.
57. *Letters: The Early Years*, I, 569.
58. *Letters: The Early Years*, I, 576.
59. *Letters: The Early Years*, I, 567.
60. *Letters: The Middle Years*, III, 76.
61. *Letters: The Middle Years*, III, 95.
62. *Letters: The Middle Years*, III, 115.
63. *Letters: The Middle Years*, III, 361.
64. Christopher Wordsworth, *Memoirs of William Wordsworth, Poet-Laureate, D.C.L.* (London, 1851), II, 476.
65. *Letters: The Middle Years*, III, 189.
66. *PW*, IV, 463.
67. Bewell, p. 196. Marcel Kessel, in "Wordsworth's 'We are Seven,' " *Explicator*, 2 (1944), 43, also insists that the girl has no intuitive knowledge.
68. *Letters: The Middle Years*, III, 32, 59, 88. There were as yet no graves in the area where the children played; see David McCracken, *Wordsworth and the Lake District: A Guide to the Poems and Their Places* (Oxford, 1984), p. 105.
69. *Letters: The Middle Years*, III, 33.
70. Bewell, p. 203. But Bewell's claim on the same page that the speaker's "vision of the afterlife . . . could hardly be cruder, or more marvelously strange and terrible" is not substantiated by the poem nor by the larger context presented by Wordsworth into which it fits.
71. With very little evidence but a great deal of speculation, Alan Bewell (p. 204) argues that the abrupt disappearance of Lucy Gray showed Wordsworth "was explicitly modeling the poem on the story of Enoch," who " 'walked with God; and he was not.' " (Wordsworth, however, clearly saw Enoch as an example of simple apotheosis—see p. 220.) He also misreads the line "And never looks behind" (surely signifying that she no longer walks in fear) to make an unnecessary and implausible connection with the Orpheus myth.

Wordsworth's Psychology of Vision: Joy, Calm, and Insight

After some fifty years of considerable scholarship dedicated to examining William Wordsworth's transcendental interests, it is no longer necessary to argue very strenuously that he is not what is usually thought of as a nature poet. That is, although Wordsworth was an admirer, even a "lover" of nature, and although nature formed a central interest in his life and works, it was not usually nature only for its own sake, but for something far beyond it. There is, in short, a strong mystical or visionary element in many of Wordsworth's poems.

Outside his poems, Wordsworth testified to the overall spirituality of his interests. To his friend, Sir George Beaumont, Wordsworth in 1805 made two pertinent comments; he called his own "habits, practises and moral notions of the world" and his own life, "altogether unworldly"; and a few months later he said he cared "so little about what the world seems to care so much for."[1]

Most of the evidence, consequently, leaves one with only the need to object to the frequently implied assumption in today's scholarship that Wordsworth's spiritual views are invalid (presumably because all spirituality is invalid in our secular age); there is often a good deal of time spent considering the biographical reasons Wordsworth thought as he did or, in the larger history of ideas, why the Romantics who shared such transcendental interests thought as they did. What we are set out to do, on the other hand, is to make no judgments about the validity of his visions but rather to look at the psychological underpinnings Wordsworth worked out for his spiritual views, for he always seems to have wished to understand the psychology behind all his involvements, even if, as with the mystical or visionary, he was unable to understand the involvements themselves.

The term *mystical* poses problems; if the word is applied strictly as Mark Schorer does to determine whether William Blake was a mystic, then Wordsworth was certainly not one.[2] And yet seeing Wordsworth in the context of the Mystical tradition brings into relief certain elements of Wordsworth's spirituality. In a recent book on Mysticism, Michael Cox seeks to define the term:

> [Mysticism] begins in a fundamental consciousness of a beyond, of a Reality, changeless and eternal, that permeates and gives meaning to the world and experiences of finite creation. The mystic in all cultures apprehends a truth that is beyond the grasp of the rational intellect: his consciousness is extended so that, in a state of

inexplicable sublimity, he grasps the abiding
unity of all things, perceiving the co-immanence
of the eternal and the temporal.[3]

This very wide definition does in fact include Wordsworth's ideas and experiences. There are the transcendental and extra-rational aspects that are clearly present
in Wordsworth, as well as a point not always recognized
by the layman, the insistence on "the abiding unity of
all things" as central to the tradition.[4]

There are other more specific similarities between
Wordsworth and the tradition as various scholars describe it. The spiritual perception that relies on organs
of sense in the soul has been dealt with in J.S.Lyons *The
Excursion: A Study* (1950).[5] There are also the mystical
process of the purgative life (the rejection of the tyranny
of the senses) and the method of theocentric contemplation (the approach to God through the visible universe).[6]
Finally, there is the passiveness and tranquility that William James lists as one of the four characteristics of the
tradition and that, as we shall see, figures largely in
Wordsworth's spiritual discipline.[7]

But perhaps after all it is safer to call Wordsworth's
transcendental experiences *visionary*. He himself seemed
to object to *mystical* with regard to analyzing the soul:
"not in a mystical and idle sense"; and he used *visionary*
himself: "Thence did I drink the visionary power."[8]
And without all the entanglements of characteristics ac-
crued over centuries by a tradition, *visionary* seems to
allow for a wider participation, the sort that Wordsworth embraces in *The Prelude*:

Points have we all of us within our souls
Where all stand single; this I feel, and make

Breathings for incommunicable powers.
Yet each man is a memory to himself,
And, therefore, now that I must quit this theme,
I am not heartless; for there's not a man
That lives who hath not had his god-like hours. . . .
                                        (1805; III, 186–92)

And he speaks much later of
Gentle awakenings, visitations meek;

A kindly influence whereof few will speak,
Though it can wet with tears the hardiest cheek.
                                        (*PW*, IV, 16)

A recent study has gone far in this same expansive
direction; by surveying autobiographies and the experiences of students, Michael Paffard discovered that many
people, especially when young, experience the same
sort of "out-of-the-ordinary states of consciousness" as
those described by Wordsworth.[9] Again, some of the details are illuminating; for example, the experiences were
felt to be ineffable, transitory, rare, unitive, valuable,
insightful, and divine and gave a sense of timelessness or
placelessness, as well as a loss of bodily sensation.[10]
Most of the experiences occurred in adolescence, dieing
off in adulthood, and typically they occurred in solitude, outside in the country, and at night. Some involved a "trance" and most a sudden uplift or relief after
uneasiness or depression.[11] Overall, the similarities to
Wordsworth's visionary experiences are quite striking.
    Such experiences, whether of the traditional mystical
sort or of the more common variety, are ineffable, but
usually, as both Cox and Paffard point out, people who
enjoy them tend to try to describe them anyway.[12]
Wordsworth, in a comment which prefaces the quota-

tion from Book III of *The Prelude* given above, describes the ineffability: "in the main, / It lies far hidden from the reach of words."

The Prelude too is a major source of the attempts he also made to uncover the necessary words beyond his reach. There are so many passages that one from Book III must suffice:

> As if awakened, summoned, rouzed, constrained,
> I looked for universal things, perused
> The common countenance of earth and heaven,
> And, turning the mind in upon itself,
> Pored, watched, expected, listened, spread my thoughts,
> And spread them with a wider creeping, felt
> Incumbences more awful, visitings
> Of the upholder, of the tranquil soul,
> Which underneath all passion lives secure
> A steadfast life. But peace, it is enough
> To notice that I was ascending now
> To such community with highest truth.
>
> . . . .
>
>   The great mass
> Lay bedded in a quickening soul, and all
> That I beheld respired with inward meaning.
> Thus much for the one presence, and the life
> Of the great whole. . . .
>   (1805; III, 109–20, 127–31)

And then beyond the experiences, Wordsworth provides a context, personal and historical:

> Such sympathies would sometimes shew themselves
> By outward gestures and by visible looks—

> Some called it madness; such indeed it was,
> If childlike fruitfulness in passing joy,
> If steady moods of thoughtfulness matured
> To inspiration, sort with such a name;
> If prophesy be madness; if things viewed
> By poets of old time, and higher up
> By the first men, earth's first inhabitants,
> May in these tutored days no more be seen
> With undisordered sight.
>
> (1805; III, 145–55)

And Wordsworth later in *The Prelude* says of such visionaries, present and past:

> They need not extraordinary calls
> To rouze them—in a world of life they live,
> By sensible impressions not enthralled,
> But quickened, rouzed, and made thereby more fit
> To hold communion with the invisible world.
> Such minds are truly from the Deity,
> For they are powers; and hence the highest bliss
> That can be known is theirs—the consciousness
> Of whom they are. . . .
>
> (1805; XIII, 101–109)

The need for a visionary to "unsensualize" his spirit (*PW*, II, 314) mentioned above, is reiterated a few lines later, where he condemns

> The tendency, too potent in itself,
> Of habit to enslave the mind—I mean
> Oppress it with the laws of vulgar sense,
> And substitute a universe of death,

The falsest of all worlds, in place of that
Which is divine and true.

(1805; XIII, 138–143)

Beyond *The Prelude*, and even beyond the obvious
relevance of "Tintern Abbey" and the "Ode: Intimations," there are constant references after 1798 to the
visionary experience; we hear of "dreams and visionary
impulses" (*PW*, II, 114), "a visionary scene" (*PW*, II,
122), "a blessed vision," (*PW*, I, 247), "visionary powers" (*PW*, V, 113), "visionary splendors" (*PW*, IV, 13),
and "visionary skill" (*PW*, II, 306). But while *The Prelude* and "Ode: Intimations" deal mainly with the vision
in youth and with its fading in adulthood, in *The Excursion* we learn, what we might have guessed, that visionary powers return in old age, which is like "a final Em-
inence," "a mountain-top" whence one gazes on a
valley below:

. . . While the gross and visible frame of things
Relinquishes its hold upon the sense,
Yea almost on the Mind herself, and seems
All unsubstantialized. . . .

The murmur of the leaves
Many and idle, visits not his ear:
This he is freed from, and from thousand notes
(Not less unceasing, not less vain than these)
By which the finer passages of sense
Are occupied; and the Soul, that would incline
To listen, is prevented or deterred.

(*IX*, 63–66, 74–80)

So the shuffling figures of old men in such poems as
"Animal Tranquility and Decay" and "The Old Cum-

berland Beggar" would seem to be within the visionary
realm by dint of the deterioration of their senses.

Not so well known are passages in various poems
composed after *The Excursion* that continue to deal with
the visionary, even if they don't present visionary experiences. In "Presentiments" (1830), Wordsworth
mentions:

> Yet there are
> Blest times when mystery is laid bare,
> Truth allows a glorious face,
> While on that isthmus which commands
> The councils of both worlds, she stands,
> Sage Spirits! by your grace.
>
> (ll. 67–72)

"Isthmus" seems in fact a better metaphor that the cur-
rently popular "border" for the separation of the everyday world and the transcendent; for "border" suggests a
rather narrow boundary easily crossed.[13]

In 1831 and again in 1833 Wordsworth refers to the
visionary unity of all: "all things blending into one"
(*PW*, III, 267) and "Till into one loved vision all things
melt" (*PW*, IV, 4). In 1835 we also hear of "things in-
ward and outward held / In such an even balance, that
the heart / Acknowledges God's grace . . ." (*PW*, IV,
276). And as late as 1842 Wordsworth talks of "all the
mysteries of our Being" (*PW*, IV, 177).

When Wordsworth spoke earlier in *The Prelude*
concerning what Paffard would call his "out-of-the-
ordinary experiences,"[14] the "spots of time" were central to his discussion. The passage where he names them
is in Book XI (1805):

There are in our existence spots of time,
Which with distinct preeminence retain
A renovating virtue, whence, depressed
By false opinion and contentious thought,
Or aught of heavier or more deadly weight
In trivial occupations and the round
Of ordinary intercourse, our minds
Are nourished and invisibly repaired. . . .
This efficacious spirit chiefly lurks
Among those passages of life in which
We have had deepest feeling that the mind
Is lord and master, and that outward sense
Is but the obedient servant of her will.
Such moments, worthy of all gratitude,
Are scattered everywhere, taking their date
From our first childhood. . . .

(ll. 257–64, 268–75)

Jonathan Bishop has argued that the "spots of time" are not "mystical" (and presumably not visionary either) but are psychological.[15] He claims that the "spots" described above are not explicitly connected with religion and that Wordsworth made no claims of transcendent insight for them.

But surely *psychological* and *visionary* are not mutually exclusive terms. Nor does Wordsworth have to make any specifically religious or transcendental claims in order for the experiences to have both those qualities. They certainly share the "unsensualized" quality (lines 270–72) with the mystical tradition and its more ordinary visionary counterpart. The unitive characteristic also shared by the two is likewise part of many of the Spots—especially that experienced in the Simplon Pass. The visionary experience, confined largely to youth and early adulthood in Paffard's study, moreover, meets with a similar age limit in *The Prelude*, for we are told in Book XII:

> . . . The hiding-places of man's power
> Open; I would approach them, but they close.
> I see by glimpses now; when age comes on,
> May scarcely see at all. . . .
>
> (ll. 279–82)

But the psychological aspect of the "spots of time" is also clearly present in their renovating retention in the mind, insisted on likewise in "Tintern Abbey" and a number of other poems. And some of the psychological conditions favoring such visionary moments were described by Wordsworth in a reported conversation with Thomas De Quincey:

> I have remarked, from my earliest days, that, if under any circumstances, the attention is energetically braced up to an act of steady observation, or of steady expectation, then, if this intense condition of vigilance should suddenly relax, at that moment any beautiful, any impressive visual object, or collection of objects, falling upon the eye, is carried to the heart with a power not known under other circumstances.[16]

In the Preface to *Poems* (1815), the psychology of this passage is applied to "There Was a Boy," when such a visionary event is represented.[17]

But there is a good deal more to the background of the visionary experience than that, and Wordsworth, partly in conjunction with Samuel Taylor Coleridge, spent an enormous amount of thought and words speculating on that background. The two key elements he repeated so many times that they are easily missed: calm and joy. And yet they are so pervasive, so often joined together, and so frequently linked with a sense of vision that a few scholars *have* remarked on them, although not giving them the sort of very great importance I believe they deserve.[18]

We have seen that passiveness or calm is a characteristic of the mystical tradition and Wordsworth scholars have noted the similarity between the tradition and Wordsworth's ideas. Newton Stallkneckt cites Jacob Boehme:

> If it be possible for (a man) to stand an hour or less from his own inner willing and speaking, then will the divine will speak into him. . . . For if the life stand still from its own will, it is in the abyss of Nature and creation, in the eternal divine utterance; and hence God speaks therein.[19]

Melvin Rader finds the same idea of passivity within Chinese mysticism, citing Chuang Tze:

> When water is still, it is like a mirror, reflecting the beard and the eyebrows. It gives the accuracy of the water-level, and the philosopher makes it his model. And if water thus derives lucidity from stillness, how much more the faculties of the mind? The mind of the sage being in repose becomes the mirror of the universe, the speculum of all creation.[20]

Both Stallkneckt and Rader discuss the connection of their respective citations with Wordsworth's views.[21]

The idea of calm appears under various names in Wordsworth's works, chiefly idleness and passivity, but it is the idea itself that is important to keep in mind. Wordsworth is not very concerned to keep the idea clear, and sometimes he seems to be attacking it, especially when it has the common pejorative sense associated with the word *idleness*, as when he is against "the strenuous idleness of worldlings." In "Gypsies," for example, he takes a gypsy encampment to task for not moving, for their "torpid life" (line 22). Wordsworth is not in favor of sloth.

Jeffrey Baker, who studied Wordsworth's idea of idleness, insists that the idleness must be deliberate (as indeed it can be), but that, I believe, is not the real distinction between good and bad idleness.[22] It is rather that the bad variety, which can also be deliberate, leads nowhere, is simply inactivity for its own sake. Baker also claims that the good state of idleness (for him the deliberate state), is not for everyone, but I don't believe Wordsworth would agree, for it seems to be the natural condition of the young and very old and seems also, as we shall see, to be bound up with the visionary experience, which he claims that all share at one time or another.[23]

There is a considerable range in the condition Wordsworth refers to as calm or passive or idle (in the good sense). It is often a heightened mental condition, an extraordinary sense of peace, as in the lines (*PW*, III, 75): "But this is calm; there cannot be / A more entire tranquility." In another, shorter poem, we have again a more than common calm (*PW*, IV, 423):

                                        The air
In the habitual silence of this wood

Is more than silent; and this bed of heath—
Where shall we find so sweet a resting-place?
Come, let me see thee sink into a dream
Of quiet thoughts, protracted till thine eye
Be calm as water when the winds are gone
And no one can tell whither.

And in a later unpublished poem, "The Tuft of Primroses," hermits are said to crave "peace / The central feeling of all happiness" (lines 274–75) and monks to yearn for

The universal instinct of repose
The longing for confirmed tranquility
In small and great, in humble and sublime,
The life where hope and memory are as one,
Earth quiet and unchanged, the human soul
Consistent in self-rule, and heaven revealed
To meditation in that quietness.

(ll. 289–95)

The mention of monasteries and meditation brings immediately to mind the New Testament story of Martha and Mary, Mary having chosen the better, though seemingly less useful, part—contemplation. It also brings to mind the mystical tradition and the fourth of William James' four characteristics, passivity.[24] For the mystical experience sometimes comes unexpectedly ("That happy stillness of the mind / Which fits him to receive [the truth] when unsought"), but mystics also prepare for it by quieting the mind.

Yet calm seems also to have been simply part of Wordsworth's way of life, the circumstances in which he was raised and in which he lived. George Sturt, writing in 1911 of a community like those existing a hundred or so years before in the Lake District, bemoans "the old lost sense of quiet."[25] He also writes of the "tranquility" and "contentment"[26] that had existed in the village whose demise he is studying,

> a community not rapidly growing in numbers, nor yet subject to crazes and sudden changes of a fashion — a community patiently, nay cheerfully, conservative in its ambitions, not given to rash speculation, but contented to go on plodding on in its time-honoured and modest well-being.[27]

Wordsworth felt there was "too much hurrying about" in the England of his day and was thankful for what the "repose and quiet" of the Lake District had done for him "through the course of a long life."[28]

A number of personal anecdotes give ample witness to Wordsworth's personal tranquility. Benjamin Robert Haydon, the painter, described him in 1815:

> I had a cast made yesterday of Wordsworth's face. He bore it like a philosopher. [John] Scott was to meet him at Breakfast. Just as he came in the plaster was covered over. Wordsworth was sitting in the other room in my dressing gown, with his hands folded, sedate, steady, & solemn. I stepped in to Scott, & told him as a curiosity to take a peep, that he might say the first sight he ever had of so great a poet was such a singular one as this.
>
> I opened the door slowly, & there he sat innocent & unconscious of our plot . . . with all the mysterious silence of a spirit.[29]

Another instance was recorded by Henry Crabb Robinson, a friend of the Wordsworths, four years later:

> . . . I was glad to accompany the Wordsworths to the British Museum. I had to wait for them in the ante-room, and we had at last but a hurried survey of the antiquities. I did not perceive that Wordsworth enjoyed much the Elgin Marbles, but he is a still man when he does enjoy himself and by no means ready to talk of his pleasure except to Miss Wordsworth.[30]

And the calm is again noticed by Ellis Yarnall, an American visitor in Wordsworth's last year:

> As we returned he walked very slowly, occasionally stopping when he said anything of importance; and again I noticed that looking into remote space of which I have already spoken.[31]

It is not hard to imagine that if Wordsworth had lived on he might well have become like one of those old men of whom he wrote in "Animal Tranquility and Decay"—the ultimate in human passivity.

In the same reminiscences, Mary Wordsworth is described as possessing what "seemed peculiarly the temper of her spirit—*peace*—the holy calmness of a heart to which Love had been 'an unerring light.' "[32] And, in fact, calm seems to have been a virtue much admired and practiced by the Wordsworth menage as a good in itself. Before Mary was part of the family, Dorothy had written to her:

> . . . Above all, my dearest Mary, seek quiet or rather amusing thoughts. Study the flowers, the

birds and all the common things that are about you. O Mary, my dear Sister! be quiet and happy.[33]

In 1813, Wordsworth himself had written to Lord Lonsdale of "that tranquility of mind which it is our duty to aim at,"[34] and in 1827 Wordsworth dispensed the following advice to an American woman who had visited him and requested help:

Let me recommend to you to observe and to read more—and to talk less—not that you do not talk well, but by silence your nerves will be enabled to recover their tone. . . . I have urged you to read more and pray do not (like the multitude) read books to talk and prattle about them, but to feed upon their contents in stillness. . . . Seek comparative solitude, till your nerves are braced. In the words of Scripture, commune with your own heart and be still—cheerfulness will then come back to you, and regaining sustained contentment will be your reward.[35]

The Wordsworths clearly took their tranquility seriously.[36]

As one might expect, Wordsworth carried this interest in tranquility for its own sake into his poetry as well. In *The Prelude,* he exclaims over "the calm existence that is mine when I / Am worthy of myself" (1805; I, 360–61) and he advises Coleridge: "Fare thee well./ Health and the quiet of a healthful mind / Attend thee, seeking oft the haunts of men . . . (1805; II, 479–81). And on the same note of overcoming the busy-ness of modern

living, he worries about contemporary educators
("watchful men / And skilful in the usury of time"):

> . . . When will they be taught
> That in the unreasoning progress of the world
> A wiser spirit is at work for us,
> A better eye than theirs, most prodigal
> Of blessings, and most studious of our good,
> Even in what seem our most unfruitful hours?
> (1805; V, 383–88)

Thus we are brought back from the simple espousal of
calm to the reasons behind that espousal, the "wise passiveness" we will turn to in a moment.

But, before that, the connection between calm or
passivity and esthetic inspiration ought to be considered. Rosamond Harding in her classic study *An Anat-
omy of Inspiration* (1940) describes the subject in much
the same way as Michael Cox treated traditional mysticism. Inspiration, like the mystical experience, comes
unsought, according to Harding, but can be prepared
for, quiet and a state of half-sleep being most propi-
tious, for indeed passivity and receptivity are necessary
for inspiration to take place.[37] In any case, however, the
inspiration must be judged later when once again
calm—a pattern reminiscent of Wordsworth's own formula in the Preface to *Lyrical Ballads* of the "spontane-
ous overflow of powerful feelings," originating in
"emotion recollected in tranquility."

When calm is linked with joy in a distinct pattern,[38]
that pattern shares with so much psychological phenomena the property of being paradoxical. For we don't
normally think of joy as being passive or tranquil; the
connotations are rather of activity and excitement.[39] For

example, when a husband writes of his feelings upon
seeing his wife after an absence we anticipate he will
speak of high emotions bubbling over, as indeed Wordsworth begins to do in a letter of 1810: "And now my
sweet and dearest love I am brought to the point where
I may allow my heart to flow over a little," but then
qualifies, "and but a little." He wishes to speak "of love
and hope and joy" and then writes unexpectedly: ". . .
the prospect of seeing my Beloved again so soon makes
me more tranquil both day & night, at least enables me
better to bear my longings, and to keep more genially
and comfortably."[40]

In the poems there is often this same paradoxical
quality. In "The Idiot Boy," for instance, we find this
stanza:

> But when the Pony moved his legs,
> Oh! then for the poor Idiot Boy!
> For joy he cannot hold the bridle,
> For joy his head and heels are idle,
> He's idle all for very joy.

(ll. 72–76)

His mother also "cannot move for joy" (line 373), although at one point she demonstrates the more conventional view of joy's effects:

> She kisses o'er and o'er again
> Him whom she loves, her Idiot Boy;
> She's happy here, is happy there,
> She is uneasy everywhere;
> Her limbs are all alive with joy.

(ll. 387–91)

But the usual paradoxical nature of the connection is reflected in the large number of oxymorons which so flourish that their tension between appearance and reality tends to be overlooked. We hear of such conditions as "calm delight," "calm revelry," "serene delight," "happy stillness," "ease and undisturbed delight," "complete composure and . . . happiness entire," and "a cheerful quiet scene." And the two conditions—calm and joy—combine often to lead to vision, as we shall see.

They have both the same sources as well; both come from Nature, as we learn in "Tintern Abbey":

> . . . 'tis her privilege,
> Through all the years of this our life, to lead
> From joy to joy: for she can so inform
> The mind that is within us, so impress
> With quietness and beauty. . . .
>
> (ll. 123–27)

In *The Prelude* we also read of "the calm / Which Nature breathes among the hills and groves" (1805; I, 284–85) and of her "never-failing principle of joy" (1805; II, 465). Nature, furthermore, is the instrument of God, who is addressed as "the giver of all joy" (1805; VI, 614). There are other instruments, such as poetry and man, but nature appears to be the central medium of joy and calm. Nature seems also even to prepare one for vision; Dorothy Wordsworth in 1803 reported an observation of her brother that a Highland boy they saw had "that visionariness which results from a communion with the unworldliness of nature."[41]

Matthew Arnold puts joy at the center of Wordsworth's greatness:

> Wordsworth's poetry is great because of the extraordinary power with which Wordsworth feels the joy offered to us in nature, the joy offered to us in the simple primary affections and duties; and because of the extraordinary power with which, in case after case, he shows us this joy, and renders it so as to make us share it.[42]

George W. Meyer, a scholar writing in 1950, also talks of Wordsworth's "Philosophy of Joy" (capitalized), but, like Arnold, Meyer makes no effort to describe it beyond very general terms; it is a given, not a matter for analysis.[43] Both are nevertheless correct in assuming the importance of joy.

Unlike calm, however, joy is not found among the characteristics of the mystical tradition, although it would certainly not, I believe, be excluded.[44] In fact in its extended meaning, joy *should* be included. Joy has, in any case, its own tradition, which has never to my knowledge been traced in Wordsworth scholarship.

Samuel Taylor Coleridge shared the concept of joy with Wordsworth during at least the years of their closest collaboration; in "Dejection: An Ode" joy performs a central role as the contrary of dejection.[45] Coleridge scholars have traced many of the possible sources of joy, although no central line has yet been established. George H. Gilpin found a source in both pagan and Christian worship of an "ecstatic nature," especially that described by Plato in the *Ion* regarding poets—Dionysian or Bacchic ecstacy.[46] George Dekker offers a wider list of sources: Christian hedonism, the World Harmony Tradition, the *Freude* of Schiller, the *joi d'amour* of the troubadors, the Psalms, seventeenth-century Neo-Platonists, Boehme, and eighteenth-century English poets and prose writers.[47] Donald Davie, writing on Wordsworth, added the *admiratio* of Aristotelian and Post-Aristotelian literary theory.[48] Dekker reinforces the feeling of no direct line being established by characterizing the concept of joy as "something partly inherited and partly worked out together by two men whose experiences of Joy and Grief were not identical. . . ."[49]

In addition to the absence of a firm tradition from which Wordsworth and Coleridge derived their concept of joy, joy, like calm, takes many names (glee, delight, happiness—usually with an intensive modifier) and signifies varied experiences.[50] Like calm again, joy and its synonyms, moreover, often take on a significance well beyond their everyday meanings. Lionel Trilling, comparing it to pleasure, saw it as "a purer and more nearly transcendent state," while Stephen Gill considers it as above "supreme well being."[51] Often Wordsworth has difficulty conveying this extraordinary joy and sometimes resorts to a modifier: "sublimer joy," "higher joy," "brighter joy," "deep enthusiastic joy," "perfect joy of heart . . . , consummate happiness." But he also often simply lets the context carry the added significance, especially in connection with vision.

There is also a connection of joy with pleasure noted by George Dekker in his study of Coleridge; Dekker calls pleasure a "near-relation."[52] Indeed, the connection is not hard to find; in the Preface to *Lyrical Ballads* Wordsworth defines the poet partly as "a man *pleased* with his own passions and volitions, and who *rejoices* more than other men in the spirit of life that is in him; *delighting* to contemplate similar volitions and passions as manifested in the goings-on of the Universe. . . ."[53] And the "pleased," "rejoices," and "delighting" begin to gather hedonistic momentum as he goes on to define the purpose of poetry as pleasure three times within the next two paragraphs, culminating in the second in "the grand elementary principle of pleasure" at the center of human life.[54] Considering that principle and the statement in *The Prelude* (1805; XIII, 147) about "the adverse principles of pain and joy," one is tempted to equate pleasure and joy, rather than see them simply as "near-relations."

But joy can exist without pleasure, as C. S. Lewis in his autobiography *Surprised by Joy* (1955) bears witness:

> . . . I will only underline the quality common to the three experiences; it is that of an unsatisfied desire which is itself more desirable than any other satisfaction. I call it Joy, which is here a technical term and must be sharply distinguished both from Happiness and from Pleasure. Joy (in my sense) has indeed one characteristic, and one only, in common with them; the fact that anyone who has experienced it will want it again. Apart from that, and considered only in its quality, it might almost equally well be called a particular kind of unhappiness or grief. But then it is the kind we want. I doubt whether anyone who has tasted it would ever, if both were in his power, exchange it for all the pleasures in the world. But then Joy is never in our power and pleasure often is.[55]

Lewis, who took the title of his book and presumably at least part of his understanding of the term *joy* from Wordsworth, is not, I believe, saying that joy is neither happy nor pleasing but only that it needn't be, although he is surely excluding sensual pleasure as a synonym for joy.

Wordsworth seems to be in general agreement, for he connects joy and sorrow in various ways, in one poem quite explicitly: "How nearly joy and sorrow are allied!" (*PW*, III, 281). In a late poem, he even seems to claim that there is a variety of "joy based on sorrow" (*PW*, IV, 130). And in an earlier unpublished fragment, probably written for the 1805 *Prelude*, he makes a curious point:

> Thus do I urge a never-ending way
> Year after year, with many a sleep between,
> Through joy and sorrow; if my lot be joy
> More joyful if it be with sorrow sooth'd.
>
> (*PW*, V, 347)

In *The Waggoner*, moreover, Wordsworth offers an idea very much like that proposed by Keats in "Ode on Melancholy":

> 'Twere worth a wise man's while to try
> The utmost anger of the sky:
> To *seek* for thoughts of a gloomy cast,
> If such the bright amends at last.
>
> (II, 72–75)

Joy of the happy variety seems also to allow for pain. In Barron Field's *Memoirs of Wordsworth*, he reported the poet as having "one day" said to him:

> "It is not enough for a poet to possess the power of mind; he must also have knowledge of the heart, and this can only be acquired by time and

tranquil leisure. No great poem has been written by a young man or by an unhappy one. It was poor dear Coleridge's constant infelicity that prevented him from being the poet that Nature had given him the power to be. He had always too much personal and domestic discontent to paint the sorrows of mankind."[56]

And then Wordsworth, in a direct reference to the following passage in *The Excursion* (I, 366–71) about the Wanderer, claimed Coleridge could *not* "afford to suffer / With those whom he saw suffer":

> . . . In himself
> Happy, and quiet in his cheerfulness,
> He had no painful pressure from within
> That made him turn aside from wretchedness
> With coward fears. He could *afford* to suffer
> With those whom he saw suffer.

In *The Prelude* (1805; X, 869–71), occurs a similar concept: "withal / A happy man, and therefore bold to look / On painful things." And the converse appears in a late poem: ". . . They best can serve true gladness / Who meet most feelingly the calls of sadness" (*PW*, III, 56).

There is present in these quotations from Wordsworth's poetry an implicit idea of balance between joy and sorrow, pleasure and pain, and I believe the idea of balance was intentional, for it also exists in his literary theory. In the Preface to *Lyrical Ballads*, Wordsworth in the passage on pleasure sees life as "an infinite complexity of pain and pleasure" and proceeds to talk of an "overbalance of enjoyment," a shock being "counterbalanced by any pleasure," "an overbalance of pleasure," and pathetic scenes being taken "beyond the bounds of pleasure."[57] This idea of overbalance is taken still further in the poems. Sorrow can become "over-charged with pain" and need relief (*PW*, IV, 257). In "Resolution and Independence" (lines 22–25), there seems to exist an exact balance:

> But, as it sometimes chanceth, from the might
> Of joy in minds that can no further go,
> As high as we have mounted in delight
> In our dejection do we sink as low. . . .

Here there is a sense of a pendulum swing from one height to another.

That upset in balance is not an unusual idea, but the upset in the direction of joy begins to shade off into paradox. For joy, Wordsworth argues, can seek "truce and rest / From her own overflow" (*PW*, III, 11) and then we find ourselves in the condition expressed in the well-known "Lines Written in Early Spring" (ll. 3–4): "In that sweet mood when pleasant thoughts / Bring sad thoughts to the mind." In the "Ode to Lycoris," Wordsworth repeats the idea (ll. 23–27):

> Sad fancies do we then affect,
> In luxury of disrespect
> To our own prodigal excess
> Of too familiar happiness.

Sometimes, however, the overbalance of joy is simply squandered, as in "Nutting" (ll. 39–43):

> . . . In that sweet mood when pleasure loves to pay
> Tribute to ease; and, of its joy secure,

> The heart luxuriates with indifferent things,
> Wasting its kindliness on stocks and stones,
> And on the vacant air.

The presence of the phrase "in that sweet mood" both here and in the quotation from "Lines" (above) suggests that Wordsworth connected the ideas of the two passages; joy and pleasure get out of balance and the excess is eliminated one way or another.

The matter of balance further suggests balancing accounts, and in fact another, mercantile metaphor appears in Wordsworth's treatment of joy. In "The Idiot Boy" the mother in a moment of pride accumulates joy and (ll. 134–36)

> Could lend out of that moment's store
> Five years of happiness or more
> To any that might need it.

We are also told in *The Prelude* that memories of the past, including a certain "delight," will stick in the mind, "whence profit may be drawn in times to come" (1805; III, 648–68). But lending from stores and drawing profits in interest are not the main part of what one is tempted to call joy-in-the-bank.

For the ability to make withdrawals of earlier experiences of joy looms large in Wordsworth's concept of joy and presents, I believe, another paradox. Wordsworth only once takes the conventional view of the likely effect of remembering past joys in present depression in a later poem entitled "Captivity—Mary Queen of Scots": "So joys, remembered without wish or will, / Sharpen the keenest edge of present ill" (lines 6–7). His standard view of joy-remembered first occurs in a letter of 1790: "At this moment when many of these landscapes are floating before my mind, I feel a high [enjoyment] in reflecting that perhaps scarce a day in my life will pass [in] which I shall not derive some happiness from these images."[58]

The best-known instances of the same phenomenon occur in "Tintern Abbey" (lines 22–30), "The Solitary Reaper" (lines 29–32) and of course "I Wandered Lonely as a Cloud" (lines 17–24), where it constitutes the theme of the poem:

> I gazed—and gazed—but little thought
> What wealth the show to me had brought;
> For oft, when on my couch I lie
> In vacant or in pensive mood,
> They flash upon that inward eye
> Which is the bliss of solitude;
> And then my heart with pleasure fills,
> And dances with the daffodils.

The future restorative quality of such moments of joy seems to link them with the "spots of time," examined earlier, but, as far as I know, no direct connection, let alone equation, was ever made by Wordsworth.

The link between calm and the visionary experience has already been made to some extent. Its best-known phrasing occurs in "Expostulation and Reply" (lines 21–24):

> Nor less I deem that there are Powers
> Which of themselves our minds impress;
> That we can feed this mind of ours
> In a wise passiveness.

But the "wise passiveness" occurs elsewhere in Wordsworth's poems; in *The Prelude*, so rife with vision, we
have (1805; II, 367–71):

> Oft in those moments such a holy calm
> Did overspread my soul that I forgot
> That I had bodily eyes, and what I saw
> Appeared like something in myself, a dream,
> A prospect in my mind.

The other link, between joy and vision, can be seen
in "The Tables Turned" (ll. 17–20), the companion piece
to "Expostulation and Reply," quoted above:

> [Nature] has a world of ready wealth,
> Our minds and hearts to bless—
> Spontaneous wisdom breathed by health,
> Truth breathed by cheerfulness.

Few Wordsworth scholars have taken much note of
this link despite its prominence; one who has noted it,
nevertheless, has considered the connection unclear.[59]
But when one turns to Coleridge scholarship, the
link is noted more widely. George H. Gilpin examines it
in several places in his study, as does George Dekker
who sums up its presence in "This Lime-tree Bower":
" 'Joy' clearly refers to a radiant moment of transensory
vision which approaches a condition of mystical union
with the divine Spirit, experienced usually—but not in-
variably—through the agency of Nature."[60] Dekker also
sees joy as, in Coleridge's view, "the great unifying and
animating principle of the universe," a view not shared
by Wordsworth despite his high regard for the condition
of joy itself.[61]

The link is strengthened in a pun on the word *genial*, which combines the two possible meanings of cheerfulness and creativity.[62] In Coleridge's "Dejection: An Ode," *genial* occurs in the phrase (line 39), "My genial spirits fail," summing up the condition of the narrator as one without "joy" and consequently without creative vision. The pun occurs a number of times in Wordsworth's poetry as well. In "Tintern Abbey" there is even a similar phrasing to Coleridge's:

> Nor perchance
> If I were not thus taught, should I the more
> Suffer my genial spirits to decay. . . .
> (ll. 111–113)

Following as it does a passage on the visionary experience, the double meaning is clear.

Likewise, in a passage in "Resolution and Independence" that analyzes his own dejection, the narrator berates his now-naive belief that "all needful things would come unsought / To genial faith, still rich in genial good . . ." (lines 38–39). The repetition of *genial* drives home the connection, when the next stanza reinforces the context of creative vision by discussing poets. Finally, in a manuscript passage intended for *The Prelude*, there occurs an attack on various evils, including

> vexing strife
> At home, and want of pleasure and repose,
> And all that eats away the genial spirits. . . .[63]

The mention of both "pleasure and repose" and the use of the same phrase ("genial spirits") seen twice above makes this an especially pertinent example.

When the three elements—calm, joy, and vision—
are joined together there occurs something like a formula, the first two elements (calm and joy) leading to
the last (vision). We see the "formula" in an early version of Coleridge's "This Lime-tree Bower" (lines
38- 40):

> Struck with joy's deepest calm
>   . . . All doth seem
> Less gross than bodily.

And in "Tintern Abbey" we find it again (lines 41–49):

>   . . . that serene and blessed mood
> In which the affections gently lead us on, —
> Until, the breath of this corporeal frame
> And even the motion of our human blood
> Almost suspended, we are laid asleep
> In body, and become a living soul:
> While with an eye made quiet by the power
> Of harmony, and the deep power of joy,
> We see into the life of things.[64]

"Quiet," "joy," and vision.

"Formula," however, hardly constitutes a system of
necessary elements. All three elements are not always
explicitly present; sometimes there are only joy and
calm or only one of the two with vision. But there are
usually at least two elements together and the other, I
believe, is never excluded, nor ever far away.

As early as revisions of *An Evening Walk* (1798?)[65] we
have phrasing very like the combination of elements: "A
mind . . . in a calm angelic mood / Of happy wisdom,
meditating good" (lines 80–81). The main location of

the combination, however, is not surprisingly *The Prelude*, the story of Wordsworth's creative vision. In the opening of Book XII (1805), we learn that Nature provides calm, and "genius" "craves / From her that happy stillness of the mind / Which fits him to receive [the truth] when unsought." And in Book VI, another short passage (lines 55–57) seems to say the same thing: "The poet's soul was with me at that time, / Sweet meditations, the still overflow / Of happiness and truth." And a hundred lines further, a longer passage contains all three elements:

Yet from this source more frequently I drew
A pleasure calm and deeper, a still sense
Of permanent and universal sway
And paramount endowment in the mind,
An image not unworthy of the one
Surpassing life, which—out of space and time,
Nor touched by welterings of passion—is,
And hath the name of, God. Transcendent peace
And silence did await upon these thoughts
That were a frequent comfort to my youth.
                                    (1805; lines 150–59)

And in Book XII again:

Oh, next to such enjoyment of our youth,
In my esteem next to such dear delight,
Was that of wandering on from day to day
Where I could meditate in peace, and find
The knowledge which I love. . . .
                                    (1805; lines 135–39)

It is mainly in these passages describing the visionary experience in a general way that joy and calm appear as part of the experience, probably because it is in the short general description that it would seem pertinent rather than in the renditions of the experiences themselves.

Calm seems to be something Wordsworth strived for; especially perhaps he deliberately sought the passivity that prepared him for vision; and even joy seems often to have been a state to arrive at by effort, if "Ode: Intimations" (strophe 3), and "At the Grave of Burns" (stanza 3) are valid evidence. Yet there are some people whose general condition seems to have the two elements of joy and calm built in, so to speak: the very young, the very old, the mentally retarded, and animals.[66]

In "The Kitten and Falling Leaves," the father-narrator speaks of "the impenetrable cell / Of the silent heart which Nature / Furnishes to every creature . . .," and he claims that "almost I could repine" that the babe's and kitten's "transports are not mine, / That I do not wholly fare / Even as ye do, thoughtless pair!" (lines 96–98, 107–110). Such passive/gleeful children and animals inhabit much of Wordsworth's poetry as do also the palsied, shuffling figures of old men, as in "Animal Tranquility and Decay," the last few lines of which would make little sense outside this context:

> He is by nature led
> To peace so perfect that the young behold
> With envy, what the Old Man hardly feels.

Or there is "The Matron of Jedborough and Her Husband," in which the latter is deaf and paralyzed and yet shares the sunshine of his joyous wife:

> ... He feels it sweet;
An animal delight though dim!
'Tis all that now remains for him!
>
> (ll. 61–63)

Or the title hero of "The Idiot Boy,"—already looked at—with his joy, idleness, and unitive insight:[67]

> "The cocks did crow to-whoo, to-whoo,
And the sun did shine so cold!"
>
> (ll. 450–51)

There is in all these conditions a feel of non–striving, an effortless compatability with the universe, which Wordsworth never quite recaptured as he travelled "farther from the east" and "into the light of common day."

Wordsworth nevertheless retained to the end an interest in the visionary, as we have seen; and there might arise a question about the possible inconsistency of his visionary views with the Christianity he was to assume shortly after the actual visionary experiences had all but ceased. One explanation might be contained in J. P. Ward's view that Wordsworth's Christianity was an "aridly-felt orthodox Anglicanism," presumably unreceptive to visionary experiences, except that this view runs counter to all the evidence.[68]

And there is an alternate explanation. Wordsworth's visionary pattern itself suggests a good deal of compatability with orthodox Christianity—the occurrence of supernatural experience and knowledge, the state of joy so often mentioned in the New Testament and in Christian liturgy, and the Christian tradition of monastic contemplation and, indeed, the Christian tradition of mysticism itself. In view of this compatability, it would in fact seem odd if the visionary element in his later works were to exist outside of, or despite, the Christianity he eventually was to embrace wholly.

There is likewise something in Christianity that allowed for a smooth transition from early non-aligned visionary experiences and for his gradual acceptance of orthodox Christianity. As Michael Cox in his study of mysticism put it: "Jesus offered a way to God, and those who followed Him could expect to be brought, like Him, to a personal consciousness of divinity. From the start, then, Christianity was an expression of man's capacity for intimate fellowship with God: it was, in other words, a fundamentally mystical religion. . . ."[69]

Or, to come at it from the other direction, there are elements of Wordsworth's earlier non-aligned spirituality that are also present in Christian tenets. It is not a great jump from his panentheism—the belief that God is all things and yet also something beyond the sum of all things—to the Christian orthodox belief that God is everywhere and yet also a spirit and person.[70] A poet of our own time, P. J. Kavanagh has, moreover, testified that his own mystical experiences or "illuminations" led him finally to Christianity, which seemed to him the natural context for his experiences, there being a place for them there as well as a tradition into which they fit.[71]

NOTES

1. Ernest de Selincourt, ed., *The Letters of William and Dorothy Wordsworth: The Early Years*, second edition, revised by Chester Shaver (Oxford, 1967), I, 554, 593. Hereafter cited as *Letters: Early Years*. Wordsworth also claimed to write *for* the "unwor[l]dly" (I, p. 400).
2. Mark Schorer, *William Blake*, (New York, 1946), chapter 3.

3. Michael Cox, *Mysticism: The Direct Experience of God* (The Aquarian Press: Wellingborough, Northamptonshire, 1983), p. 19.

4. See also Jacomina Kortelling, *Mysticism in Blake and Wordsworth*, reprint ed. (New York, 1966, originally published 1928), p. 3. R. C. Zaekner, *Mysticism Sacred and Profane* (Oxford, 1957), p. 35, claimed that Wordsworth had no unitive experiences, but Zaekner seems to have based this opinion on one passage from "Tintern Abbey."

5. pp. 97–104. Organs of the Sense are one of three fundamental articles of Christian mysticism in the view of W. R. Inge, *Christian Mysticism* (London, 1899), p. 6.

6. Cox, pp. 27, 35.

7. William James, *Varities of Religious Experience* (New York, 1902), pp. 381–82.

8. Jonathan Wordsworth et al, eds., *William Wordsworth: The Prelude* (New York and London, 1979), pp.76, 82 (1805 version; II, 234, 330). Quotations from *The Prelude* will be taken from this edition and will be cited in the text.

9. Michael Paffard, *Inglorious Wordsworths: A Study of Some Transcendental Experiences in Childhood and Adolescence* (London: Hodder and Stoughten, 1973), p. 11. See Cox, p. 17, for agreement on the wide extent of such experiences.

10. Paffard, chapter 3.

11. Paffard, chapter 10.

12. Cox, p. 23; Paffard, p. 129.

13. "Border" was originally used by Kenneth Johnston (in "The Idiom of Vision," in *New Perspectives in Coleridge and Wordsworth*, ed. G. Hartman [New York and London, 1972], p. 9) and subsequently taken over by Jonathan Wordsworth, *William Wordsworth: The Borders of Vision* (Clarendon Press, Oxford, 1982).

14. Paffard, p. 11.

15. Jonathan Bishop, "Wordsworth and the 'Spots of Time,' " *English Literary History*, 26 (1959), 147.

16. Thomas De quincey, *Literary Reminiscences* (Boston, 1854), p. 308.

17. W. J. B. Owen and J. W. Smyser, eds., *The Prose Works of William Wordsworth* (Oxford: Clarendon Press, 1974), III, 35.

18. Donald Davie, ed., *Selected Poems of William Wordsworth* (London, 1962), pp. 15–17, 25–26; Stephen C. Gill, "Wordsworth's 'Never Failing Principle of Joy,' " *English Literary History*, 34 (1967), 208–212. I also pointed out the relationship between the elements earlier in "Coleridge's 'Dejection: An Ode,' " *English Studies*, 52 (April 1971), 1.

19. Newton P. Stallkneckt, *Strange Seas of Thought* (Bloomington, Ind., 1958), p. 54.

20. Melvin Rader, *Wordsworth, A Philosophical Approach* (Oxford, 1967), pp. 131–32.

21. Archibald Alison (*Essays on the Nature and Principles of Taste* [London, 1790], facs. ed. [Heldesheim, 1968], pp. 6, 13–14, 42) also tells of a passive state mostly found in youth.

22. Jeffrey Baker, "Wordsworth's Doctrine of the Necessity of Idleness," *Criticism*, 13 (1971), 243.

23. Baker, p. 242.

24. James, pp. 381–82.

25. George Sturt (pseud. George Bourne), *Change in the Village* (London, 1912), p. 8.

26. Sturt, pp. 125–25, 120.

27. Sturt, pp. 155–56.

28. Owen and Smyser, III, 355.

29. W. B. Pope, ed., *The Journals of Benjamin Robert Haydon* (Cambridge, Mass., 1960), I, 450.

30. Edith J. Morley, ed., *Henry Crabb Robinson on Books and Their Writers* (London, 1938), I, 257.

31. Ellis Yarnall, *Wordsworth and the Coleridges* (New York, 1899), p. 45. The testimony of natives in the Lake District twenty years after Wordsworth's death tends to emphasize his calmness: a "quiet man"; "a silent man wi'out a doubt" (p. 17); "a verra quiet man, particlar quiet" (p. 31); "a very temperate man i' all things" (p. 35); see H. D. Rawnsley, *Reminiscences of Wordsworth among the Peasantry of Westmoreland* (London, 1968). Thomas De Quincey called Wordsworth the "most meditative man of his age," *Literary Reminiscences*, p. 302.

32. Yarnall, p. 41.

33. *Letters: Early Years*, I, 350.

34. Ernest de Selincourt, ed., *The Letters of William and Dorothy Wordsworth: The Middle Years, Part II*, second edition, revised by Mary Moorman and Alan G. Hill (Oxford, 1970), III, 66. (Hereafter cited as *Letters: The Middle Years, Part II*.)

35. Ernest de Selincourt, ed., *The Letters of William and Dorothy Wordsworth: The Later Years, Part I*, second edition, revised, arranged and edited by Alan G. Hill (Oxford, 1978), IV [misprinted III], 541–42. Hereafter cited as *Letters: The Later Years, Part I*.

36. The desire for tranquility could, of course, be part of Wordsworth's Roman-based stoicism; see Jane Worthington, *Wordsworth's Reading*

of Roman Prose (New Haven, 1946), pp. 62, 66–67. See also *The Prelude* (1805), X, 152–57, for a passage that seems to suggest repose of a stoic nature, as also the sonnet beginning: "Tranquility! the Sovereign aim wert thou / In heathen schools of philosophic lore . . ." (*PW*, IV, 46).

37. p. 95.

38. Rather than connect calm with joy, James Averill in his study of Wordsworth's relations with the Eighteenth-century sentimental tradition (*Wordsworth and the Poetry of Human Suffering* [Ithaca, NY, 1980], pp. 13, 85, 87, 101) discovers a pattern of connections of calm with suffering, excitement, sublimity—indeed, with strong emotions of all kinds—calm being seen in fact as a response to the emotion. Averill makes no connection between the pattern and the earlier tradition but rather sees it as a Wordsworthian phenomenon. But I believe the pattern goes well beyond Wordsworth to human nature itself; for strong emotions are *by nature* tiring and bring on repose; rest naturally follows activity. The same pattern was discovered earlier by Gilbert T. Dunklin, "Wordsworth's Voice of Calm," *Princeton University Library Chron.*, 11 (1950), 76–88. Kenneth Johnston, in "The Idiom of Vision," in *New Perspectives in Coleridge and Wordsworth*, ed. G. Hartman (New York and London, 1972), p. 24, analyzes "A Night-Piece" and likewise sees a movement from ecstasy to meditative calm. David Rogers, on the other hand, claims Wordsworth's repose "*produces* a feeling of contentment and joy" (italics added); see "The Wordsworthian Repose," *Tennessee Studies in Literature*, 13 (1968), 40.

39. The link between calm and joy was first made in Davie, *Selected Poems*, p. 16.

40. Beth Darlington, ed. *The Love Letters of William and Mary Wordsworth* (London, 1982), p. 89.

41. Ernest de Selincourt, ed., *Journals of Dorothy Wordsworth* (New York, 1941), I, 286.

42. Matthew Arnold, *Essays in Criticism, Second Series* (London, 1888), p. 153.

43. George W. Meyer, "*Resolution and Independence*: Wordsworth's Answer to Coleridge's *Dejection: An Ode*," *Tulane Studies in English*, 2 (1950), 55.

44. P. G. Stanwood in "'Essentiall Joye' in Donne's Anniversaries," in *Essential Articles for the Study of John Donne's Poetry*, ed., John R. Roberts (Handen, Connecticut, 1975), p. 392, identifies "joye" in Donne's "The Progres of the Soule," line 384, as the beatific vi-

sion, thus unifying the joy and vision of the mystics, perhaps even of Wordsworth.

45. George Dekker, in *Coleridge and the Literature of Sensibility* (London: Vision Press, 1978), p. 149, claims they agreed in 1802.

46. George H. Gilpin, *The Strategy of Joy: An Essay on the Poetry of Samuel Taylor Coleridge* (Salzburg, 1972), pp. 28–29.

47. Dekker, pp. 142, 146, 152–66.

48. Donald Davie, "Dionysius in *Lyrical Ballads*," in *Wordsworth's Mind and Art*, ed. A. W. Thomson (Edinburgh, 1969), pp. 110–39.

49. Dekker, p. 146. Spinoza is another possible source; in his *Ethic* (Third Part), joy becomes a constant contrast to sorrow as origins of "affects"; see Melvin Rader, *Wordsworth: A Philosophical Approach* (Oxford, 1967), p. 62.

50. See Dekker, p. 145. See also Jack Lee Rhodes, "A Study in the Vocabulary of English Romanticism: 'Joy' in the Poetry of Blake, Wordsworth, Coleridge, Shelley, Keats, and Byron," unpub. Doctoral Dissertation, University of Texas (1966), chapter II. Rhodes examines Wordsworth's use of the word *joy* and illustrates the many meanings it was made to bear.

51. Lionel Trilling, "The Fate of Pleasure," in *Romanticism Reconsidered*, ed. Northrup Frye (New York, 1963), p. 77. Stephen C. Gill, "Wordsworth's 'Never Failing Principle of Joy,' " *English Literary History*, 34 (1967), 210.

52. Dekker, p. 142.

53. Owen and Smyser, I, 138 (italics added).

54. Owen and Smyser, I, 140. A note to the passage identifies the idea of the source of pleasure as a "universal motive" as originating in John Dennis. See Chapter 4 above.

55. C. S. Lewis, *Surprised by Joy* (London, 1955), pp. 23–24.

56. Geoffrey Little, ed., *Barron Field's Memoirs of Wordsworth* (Sydney: Sydney University Press for Australian Academy of the Humanities, Monograph 3, 1975), p. 100.

57. Owen and Smyser, I, 140, 145, 147. There is some question of the possible influence of David Hartley on this point; see Chapter 2 above.

58. *Letters: Early Years*, I, 36.

59. Gill, pp. 209–10.

60. Gilpin, pp. 27, 33, 60; Dekker, p. 144.

61. Dekker, p. 146.

62. This pun was noted in my edition, *William Wordsworth: Poems* (Penguin Books, 1977), I, 954. The pun is also considered at some length in Dekker, pp. 168–74.

63. Jonathan Wordsworth et al, eds., *The Prelude*, p. 500.
64. Passage quoted in this regard in my "Coleridge's 'Dejection: An Ode,'" *English Studies*, 52 (April 1971), 1; also quoted by Gill (p. 209) to connect joy and vision.
65. This version is always dated 1794, but for reasons given in my article in *Studies in Bibliography* ("The Dating of the '1794' Version of Wordsworth's *An Evening Walk*," LXII [1989], 265–71), I believe it is more likely to have been written in 1798 or shortly before, or even possibly as late as 1820.
66. Alan Bewell, throughout his *Wordsworth and the Enlightenment* (New Haven, 1989), argues that Wordsworth dealt with these groups (he calls them "marginals") for another reason: he is reacting to their treatment by eighteenth-century "anthropologists." And yet he argues that Wordsworth's treatment differs from theirs in at least ten profoundly distinctive ways (pp. 30–47, 58). One wonders at what point such "displaced" and "submerged" connections seem forced and implausible, especially when based on such meager evidence and such a tenuous argument.
67. Bewell (p. 69) finds Johnny's answer "nonsensical" and otherwise misreads the ending of the poem by relying on "anthropological" explications.
68. J. P. Ward, "Wordsworth and the Sociological Idea," *Critical Quarterly*, 16 (1974), 332.
69. Cox, p. 40.
70. A similar view is expressed by Carl Woodring in *Wordsworth* (Boston, 1965), p. 106.
71. Television interview of P. J. Kavanagh by Eric Robson, on "Revelations," channel four, London, England, Saturday, October 13, 1984.

INDEX

I
Persons

II
Wordsworth's Poetry and Prose